The Power Pyramid

The Tip of the Pyramid

These foods should be eaten sparingly. You can eat fats, meat, fish, poultry, beans, and dairy at lunch and dinner. Eat these foods in small portions. Do not overdo on meats and dairy.

The Center of the Pyramid

This section is for whole grains only. A grain kernel is comprised of three layers: the bran (the outside layer where most of the fiber exists), the endosperm (a starchy middle layer) and the germ (the inside layer where many nutrients and essential fatty acids are). Manufacturers of bread and other products made of grains not only refine the grains by removing the bran and the germ, but they add sugar and yeast which are not on this diet. You can have any grains as long as they are in the whole condition. These include corn, quinoa, kamut, brown rice, etc. It's best to buy organic grains only to avoid the pesticides used when farming grains. Do not eat any bread or flour products. (See page 118)

The Bottom of the Pyramid

Eat all the fruits and vegetables you want. Any fruit or vegetable is fine and organic is even better. For Diabetic and Candida patients, check with your doctor for sugar restriction requirements.

Think of all the money you will save not buying the other "Garbage" not on this list! And don't forget the improved health, energy, and that feeling of well being.

The third edition is a clarification on the positions of the World's Major Religions: Judaism, Christianity, and Islam with regard to diet. The source of this in formation is obtained from The Old Testament, The New Testament, and the Koran. The Biblical commandments are remarkably similar. In the past, religious people continued to follow the same rules.

However, today the vast majority due to ignorance and customs do not attach the importance of the Biblical Dietary Commandments, which are really health laws. Our present standard American diet has been the result of marketing of the "products" that we find in the food markets today. This is a far cry from the diet that was originally recommended.

This edition will outline a way we can come back to the original plan, to regain the health we are entitled to and stamp out for good the degenerative diseases that plague our people today.

To do this will take the cooperation of many people including the religious leaders who will tell the people what changes would be in their own interests. There would be many hurdles to overcome and the road to recovery will be easy for some, but not for others. Food manufacturers will alter their "products" to healthy acceptable nutritious foods. Government authorities will enact stringent laws to enforce the strict requirements. We will have to destroy all the harmful foods that were the culprits that depleted our nutritional needs. There is sure to be some resistance. Food manufacturing companies will be reluctant to make changes. Also people who are addicted very strongly to certain foods will balk.

However, if we want to live long and healthy lives, our path is clear. Follow the Bible's dietary laws which are offered in this book, and your good health is assured.

The Biblical Dietary Commandments

I give you every seed bearing plant on the face of the whole earth and every tree has fruit with seed in it. That will be yours for food.
(Genesis 1:29 NIV)

The meat of animals with a cloven or split hoof and also the chew of the cud (Lev 11:3) can be eaten. This includes cows, goats, sheep, oxen, deer, buffalo and so forth.

Avoid animals such as camel that chew the cud but do not have cloven or split hooves. (Lev 11:4) This includes but not limited to horses, rats, skunks, dogs, cats, squirrels and possums.

Do not eat swine. (Pigs) They have divided hooves but they do not chew the cud. These are unclean animals. (Lev. 11:7) In fact pigs are so unclean that god warns us not to even touch the body, meat or carcass of a pig. The Hebrew words used to describe unclean meats can be translated as "foul, polluted, putrid". The same terms were used to describe "Human Waste" and other disgusting substances.

Eat any fish with fins and scales but avoid fish or water creatures *without* them. (Lev. 11:9-10) Those to avoid include smooth- skinned species such as catfish or eel and hardshelled crustaceans such as crab, lobster, or clams.

Birds that live primarily on insects, grubs, or grains are considered clean, but avoid birds or fowl that eat flesh (whether caught live or carrion). They are unclean. (see the extensive list in Leviticus 11:13-19)

From feedback I've had from readers and reviewers, there were several questions which needed to be answered. After a successful run of the First Edition, this will help to answer some of these questions.

About 5 years ago, I had a heart attack which landed me in the hospital for a few days. This gave me time to think about what led me up to this event. I was always interested in health, ate pretty well (I thought), did a lot of activities, even dancing and marathon running. So why ME? This heart attack was the wake up call that gave me the inclination to write the book, for at last I knew what had done me in.

My diet at the time was typical American. Standard American Diet (SAD) with the usual parties all of the time, with all the goodies consumed. I figured that with all of the activities I was doing, it would "burn off." Boy, was I wrong. The body is a very resilient machine and can handle some abuse, but when accumulative toxins reach the point where it cannot tolerate any more, the breakdown occurs and something's gotta give. In my case, it was a heart attack and I got the message. I realized at this time what had caused this event and what needed to change in my lifestyle to gain back my health. I don't intend to go back to my old ways again. This book is written to inform people of a healthy lifestyle.

-Max Sturman

No Sugar No Flour

Will Give ME the Power

The Lifestyle I Can Live With

Third Edition

Introduction

Dennis Goodman, M.D., F.A.C.C.

CHIEF OF CARDIOLOGY
SCRIPPS MEMORIAL HOSPITAL
LA JOLLA, CALIFORNIA

Foreword by Nancy Appleton, Ph.D.

Max Sturman

This is a non-profit venture.
That's it! - pure and simple.
There is no solicitation of any kind,
and you may reproduce anything in this book.

Give this book to someone who will benefit
from this information. Pass it along.

Health is the only true wealth.

Published by
Do It Naturally Foundation
A Nonprofit Organization
5236 Cole Street
San Diego, CA 92117

This book is dedicated to

James Hervey Johnson

One of the pioneers who, in collaboration with Dr. Herbert Shelton, began the Natural Health movement in our country. We are indebted to Mr. Johnson as he unselfishly gave of himself to further the cause of rational thinking and helped revise the eating habits and lifestyle changes to improve the health of our people today.

Contents

Chapter 1
The Lifestyle You Can Live With

Chapter 2
Supporting Factors

Chapter 4

<u>There is Hope</u>

Chapter 5

<u>Research</u>

Chapter 6

<u>Letters of Reference & Articles About Author</u>

Chapter 7

<u>Recipes</u>

Chapter 8

Thank You

I wish to thank all those people who made this book possible. Without their help and support this could not have been done.

Dr. Dennis Goodman

Nancy Appleton, a friend indeed. My "press agent" and brother, George Sturman. Jonathan Harris, my lawyer and close friend. Chriss Cornish, my right hand typist and Jenny Spencer and Nomi Levy. Margo Jackson and Andrea Glass my trusty worthy editors. My gym-mates who had the confidence to follow the lifestyle and report regularly on their progress. Their overwhelming satisfaction in attaining the goals and feeling of well-being. This reassurance motivated me to attain all the research and data pertaining to the subject.

I wish to thank the following doctors, organizations and individuals for their input and for their valuable time spent helping me: Dr. Ed Brantz, Dr. Jeffery Mazin, Dr. Joseph Mercola, Dr. Ed Omens, Dr. Jack Reingold, Dr. Michael Simons, Dr. John Vaughan. Dr Steve Gottlieb.

James Hervey Johnson Charitable Educational Trust.

The Delacruz Design Agency: Phillip Delacruz and staff, The Optimum Health Institute, 24 Hour Fitness, Carlos Aguilar and the UPS Staff, Scott Burke, Wilma Korab, John Chavez, Catharine Lee, Assemblywoman Lori Saldaña, Joe Wasyl (my best salesman), Linda Porter of *Penny Saver*, Jack Williams & Logan Jenkins of the *Union Tribune*, Jen Allbritton, Certified Nutritionist, author of *Wheaty Indiscretions*. Thomas Smith and his studies on diabetes. David Yates, Emily Reed and The UPS Store.

And my daughter, sons and grandchildren;
Andy, Neil, Joan, Nicole, Michael and Diane.

Thank you God

for the inspiration to write this book.

Introduction

Dr. Dennis Goodman
M.D, F.A.C.C.
La Jolla, California

USA Today recently reported, "Americans are eating significantly bigger portions of fries, chips, and burgers and drinking more soda than they did 20 years ago." Restaurants are serving bigger and bigger portions to customers most of whom finish what is on their plate. It is no surprise then, that 120 million Americans (>50%) are overweight or obese.

Hundreds of books have been written and billions of dollars have been spent on advertising weight reduction programs-often quick fix, fad diets that are non-sustainable and themselves unhealthy. Many of these books are complicated and their recommended diets impractical.

In contrast this author has come up with a simple, practical approach not only to weight reduction but more importantly an overall approach to being healthy.

He promotes a healthy diet, exercise program, stress management and good communication with health care providers. This all comes together as a great recipe for wellness.

He is a remarkable 88-year old gentleman who practices what he preaches. He looks 20 years younger than his age and epitomizes a healthy, well-balanced octogenarian who sets the standard for all of us, no matter your age. He has boundless energy and loves to help others, constantly giving free advice and gleaning such pleasure from people who follow his diet and recommendations for healthy living.

A tenet of his diet is avoidance of sugars in our diet. I cannot agree with him more. This in conjunction with fresh fruit and vegetables (he even has his own organic garden), moderate amounts of carbohydrates, fat and protein plus daily exercise and an overall positive approach to life is a fresh simple recipe for healthy living.

I commend him for his wonderful, simple book. It is an

honor to be his cardiologist. It makes my job with him so easy "like an early morning walk in the park" with a "juicy fresh watermelon for breakfast".

Preface

My interest in diet related topics came to a head after reading a book by Nancy Appleton, *Lick the Sugar Habit*. It had a profound effect on me as I related to the ailments described in the book. Now I know why I didn't feel as well or have the energy I wanted. I tried changing all my eating habits, but it wasn't easy. After many attempts and failures I realized I necded help. I was fortunate in meeting a qualified hypno-therapist and after one session I was on track and stuck to my diet. It was what changcd my life. I had a wonderful improvement in my feeling of well being. The other bonus was I lost a lot of excess weight and inches.

Nancy Appleton has become my mentor, and I arranged for her to give lectures locally in San Diego. She is a very popular speaker and has lectured all over the world. She has written several books and has a Ph.D. in clinical nutrition. I am privileged to know her as a friend. An article written by Jack Williams, a syndicated columnist for the San Diego Union Tribune, on July 14th of 2003 resulted in an avalanche of letters requesting my book, Do It Naturally: *The Diet You Can Live With*, and reinforced my belief I was on the right track. I realized people were seeking a better way to live and were searching for ways to improve their well being and to lose weight. This book will give you a cross-section of people who are in search of good health.

Because everyone is different, the response to the recommended Food Plan and lifestyle change varies. Some, because they had seen other people's successes in weight loss, and general feelings of well being, took to the diet immediately and without any coaxing. However, there were some who were stubborn and couldn't break their habits.

Let's get this straight. This Food Plan is easy to understand with simple rules to follow. We won't be using terms such as "carbohydrates," "proteins" or "fats." I have found that not being specific about what food we are talking about will lead to confusion and we don't want that. You'll find this makes other diet programs obsolete. You'll notice that there are no big words, just simple down to earth language that everyone understands.
But don't let all this simplicity fool you. This is a very effective and safe program with no side effects usually caused by "products." You will be eating natural foods

that the body craves and eliminating those foods that are not friendly to the body. It's as simple as that. You can expect certain changes in one week.

1. You will have a feeling of well being
2. You will lose weight and belly size
3. Complexion will clear
4. Digestion will improve
5. You will have more energy
6. Some chronic conditions will disappear
7. You will have the confidence that you are now on the right track and that you have found a new way of life. You will have no intention of ever returning to those lousy feelings caused by those poor eating habits you used to have.

You have now discovered a new way to live that works for you and you know now that this is the way you are going to do it from now on. This is not a matter of just losing weight. This is a whole lifestyle program you know works. You'll be looking at food in an entirely different way, and you won't be thinking of anything going into your mouth that will harm you. With this diet you will know the secret of a long, full and healthful life without the usual aches and pains associated with growing older. That's all you need. A one-week trial will convince you.

And it isn't hard. There is such a variety of foods you can eat. There is no need to be hungry. You may eat any fruit, vegetable, meat, fish and eggs "in reasonable quantity." At this time you may eat liberally. Eventually you'll be satisfied with smaller meals.

This is the key to success in this weight reduction program. However, if there is a need to gain weight, increased input is in order.

While waiting in line at the supermarket, I discovered it was a busy time of the day. There were unusually long lines, and I wondered why. Everyone had loaded up cases of beer and soda...many taking several huge cartons. I asked the lady, "Why is everyone buying up all this beer and soda?" She said, "Haven't you heard, they're having a big sale now! Better get yours before they run out!" I wondered what luck I would have in offering my book to these people- or if they would even read it, even if it was free. And how many would follow the Food Plan? And how many would reject it? What would it take to get people to try it just for one week? It would take cooperation from many sources: Government, Media, AMA, heart and diabetic associations, political groups, MADD, juvenile police, or any other related group that would give such endorsements for implementation.

The need to educate the public in this matter is vital at this time. Marketing people could help considerably. Remember 50 years ago, doctors would endorse cigarette advertisements, saying smoking was good for your throat and for your relaxation.

It's in your hands. You have your choice. You can eat smaller, sensible meals and lose weight, or continue to eat large meals and gain. This is the decision you – and only you – have to make. When food is placed in front of you, you must think of its value to fill your needs. Is it good nutrition or just comfort food? How much nutrition and how much comfort do you need? You can choose your well being, or your downfall, by how much you consume. Think self-control.

Max Sturman

Foreword

Nancy Appleton PhD.

Max Sturman has written an easy-to-read book on what causes disease and how to make changes to keep you healthy or improve your health. The steps are simple to follow. He has included recipes to make the transition uncomplicated. Follow his advice and you have nothing to lose but weight and symptoms and everything to gain in terms of health. And so dear reader, read on to improve your health.

Nancy Appleton, Ph.D. author of *Lick the Sugar Habit* and *Lick the Sugar Habit Sugar Counter*. Learn more at: *www.nancyappleton.com*

Chapter 1

The Lifestyle You Can Live With

What's So Different About This Lifestyle?

We are a non-profit venture and are not selling anything, we are free to be up front without any restriction that other diets impose.

We have a well researched program, taken from renowned sources like Shelton, Atkins, Ornish, Chopra, Appleton, Johnson, and many others.

I have selected those segments from these sources that I deem appropriate. The diet is indeed very easy to follow, without the need of any additional product. I have purposely made it so flexible, the simple instructions are easy to remember rules. Make this a most successful adventure to experience.

It's As Easy As That!

I've seen some big bellies in my time. Always in my mind was the belly that would not go away. It was something that I took for granted, and thought I had to live with the rest of my life. What was the big deal, anyway. Every guy I knew and those I didn't know had the same thing more or less.

Some guys and gals are lucky and didn't have the problem, so I figured it must be the genes . . . or vigorous exercise that got them in good shape. So as the years went by the belly problem was dealt with by trying to fast . . . or starving and denying myself various foods I craved.

Nothing helped as I returned to eating "normal" again. I visited a health spa one day and spent a week there. It was a real education for me. There were daily lectures. They emphasized eating slowly to help the digestive process together with anatomy, physiology and emotional control.

After a week there, I noticed my weight and belly went down a bit, but after starting to eat "normal" again, everything went back to where it was before. Weight and belly returned to its previous proportions for good. The Atkins diet drew my interest and I read the book, which seemed to make a lot of sense. I tried to follow faithfully all the steps to reach my goal. Got some positive results and felt I was on the right track.

You see, most diets are too hard and restrictive to keep up for any length of time . . . especially denying foods you are used to and crave.

So I thought if there was an uncomplicated diet, with no pills that would result in quick and harmless reduction of weight and belly size, one would be motivated to continue the diet also while eating delicious food.

Here at last I came to ponder a combination and modification of various factors that would indeed work:

1. Daily diet adherence is required for success in this program **but it doesn't have to be hard**.
2. One needs emotional stability **but it doesn't have to be hard**.
3. Exercise is a must everyday **but it doesn't have to be hard**.

On this diet you will gradually be satisfied with less food . . . which is the key to losing weight and belly proportions. All my life I've pondered what can I do to keep the weight and belly down

What's In the Belly That Weighs So Much
And How Did It Get That Way?

If you think about it you guess it's all fat, but it's not what you think. It was all caused by what we ate and what we didn't get eliminated. You see, in the intestinal tract where food goes through have villi — these ridge-like surfaces are not smooth, but are hill and dale throughout the digestive system.

Certain foods are easily digestible and naturally go through the system. However, those foods that do not are the culprits that cause a sticky glue-like substance to stick firmly in the villi and accumulate the waste that does not eliminate as it should and stays a long time.

White flour and white sugar are some of the culprits and they are to be out of your diet in any form.

The Basic Lifestyle

1. Breakfast: slice of watermelon or any other single fruit, eat as much as you want (within reason). NOTHING ELSE.

2. Lunch: Any salad, meat, fish, eggs, cheese, raw fruit and vegetable (within reason).

3. Dinner: meat, fish, eggs, cheese, raw fresh fruits and vegetables (within reason).
Optional dessert: cheese, tapioca, fruit
We do not eat bread, cake, pie, cookies, candies, sugary puddings, or other products containing white flour and/or white sugar.

If you follow this diet, you will find yourself eating less food and feeling satisfied with a feeling of well-being.

We don't eat processed food with preservatives, and overly-spicy or salty food. Water is the best beverage. Learn combinations of food that are friendly to your body.

Diet B for Diabetes and Hypoglycemia

Because of high sugar content of fruits, diabetic folk and hypoglycemics will need to substitute vegetables instead of the fruit for breakfast. However, some limited amounts of fruit are permissible.

On this diet, if followed strictly, you will find your need for insulin medication greatly diminished, and eventually completely gone for some!

It makes sense, when you stop eating the wrong foods that have caused this metabolism malfunction, nature once again, rebuilds and repairs the immune system and gets you back on track again. Check with your doctor.

Sugar Note for Candida, Sugarholics and Others

A note about sugar for people with yeast infections, Candida Albicans and sugarholics. It is a good health move for you to give up sugar for at least 2 months. This gives your body a rest and a chance to heal. So go sugar free, including fruits and fruit juices, for 2 months. Then reintroduce fruits into your diet.

No-Nos!

Breads, cake, pie, cookies, candy, pancakes, waffles, flour tortillas, puddings (store-bought), cereals and any processed foods. Foods containing white flour and white sugar. Sodas, wines, beer, hard liquor, breaded foods, syrups, canned fruit, coffee, any empty calories, artificial sweeteners, white rice. Watch out for high-fructose corn syrup, and related sugars. Ice cream, pizza, pasta or jello. Preservates: nitrites, sulfites.

Okay Foods

All fruits and vegetables, avocados, olives, eggs, meat, fish, poultry, nuts, corn tortillas, soups, 100% whole grains, wheat, rice, barley, buckwheat, etc (this does not mean bread). 100% natural peanut butter, applesauce, beans, olive oil, butter, cheese, water and tapioca. As to: corn, brown rice and potatoes, use sparingly. Be sure to remove all fat from the meat before cooking. (This is not a complete list.)

For The Children

A child's total diet and his or her activity level both play an important role in determining a child's weight. Our kids are getting set up now for problems with obesity, heart disease, diabetes or cancer later on in life. Our number one objective should be to find ways to get kids active and fit. Our schools need to be creative in making physical education fun and educational. We need to teach life skills not just run laps. The societies of the world are beginning to realize that exercise and physical education is important to the complete individual as in body, mind, and soul. Extrapolated from a paper by Peter J. Manosh, MBA Expert of Food Science, Human Nutrition, Exercise & Sport Science.

This food plan is healthy for children as well as adults. Take family nature walks to encourage the whole family in getting fit and healthy.

Exercise

For this lifestyle to be successful you must exercise every day. It is not important what form your exercise takes, as long as it's not too hard to do. Some people are of the opinion "no pain, no gain." With such an attitude, people have done more harm to themselves with dire results.

Many options are open to you. And about an hour a day is good for you. And remember, **it doesn't have to be hard**. The following suggestions are, by far, not complete. Check with your doctor: Walking, jogging, swimming, yoga, tai-chi, pilates, dancing, gardening, house-cleaning, aerobic exercise, light weights, dumbbells, video exercises, sit-ups, biking and treadmill machines.

Diet without exercise won't work. You must do both. Watch the weight disappear, watch the belly disappear. People will notice your new shape.

Want To Shout It To The World

I have discovered my cure for the common cold. It took a guinea pig . . . Me. You see this is the first time in my life that a whole year has gone by, and I did not get a cold. All my life I remember the misery I endured, the awful tasting medicine I had to take. As a child I was forced to open my mouth to get it in.

The pills, the shots, the antibiotics. The stays in bed for days, and as an adult this continued suffering occurred every year of my life when the 'season" came. The regular visits to the doctor's office, with the waiting room overstuffed with people sneezing and wheezing. The waiting often took over two-hours . . . then the good doctor would examine and diagnose my ailment and give me a prescription. Some of these ailments were, colds, flu, sore throat, ear-ache, chronic cough, etc.

This is the ritual that I had endured annually for 84 years, but not my 85th year. You see I have now discovered my cure for the common cold, and have not had a cold for a whole year. What medicine did I take? Was it a new pill? No sorry, there is no magic pill. Just a change in my lifestyle. And what was this change?

1.   The "No Sugar No Flour Diet"

2.   Daily exercise. 1 hour minimum.

It's as simple as that.

The amazing thing of this lifestyle change was, it was not hard to do. I lost a lot of unwanted weight, had increased energy and endurance, and enjoyed life more in general. Stress was now easier to handle. If this worked for me, it can work for you too!

A one-week trial on this food plan and lifestyle change will convince you. The next time you say, "I think I'm coming down with a cold," think, was it caused by being in a large crowded party? Or some baby you held, or maybe you shook hands with someone, or whatever? Not necessarily.

Maybe it was that piece of cake washed down with soda, 6 months ago. Or the time you ate the whole container of ice cream in a weaker moment last year? Or maybe it was that big party where we all had such a good time eating and drinking, without a care in the world? Improper eating and drinking will weaken your immune system and leave you more vulnerable to illness.

Testimonials #1

Fred (a scientist). . . tried every diet that came around, including daily heavy exercise. The belly just wouldn't go down. He promised he would try this diet for a week, and if he saw results would continue. He was weighing himself every day, and to his amazement, the weight went down. Of course, he continued...

1.　　First month – 10 pounds down

2.　　Second month – 10 pounds down

3.　　Third month – 10 pounds down

Fred had knee problems prior to going on the diet, which would have necessitated an operation. With 30 pounds less weight to carry, the knee problem vanished, and energy he never knew before now enhanced his life. He could now play and keep up with his kids as never before. Fred is elated about his progress, and is continuing on the program as he has another 15 pounds to reach his goal. Fred has lost 40 pounds in four months.

Tom (a disbeliever) . . . but when he saw the startling

results of Fred, he started the program. Tom's problems were many. Painful arthritis and back problems made life miserable, and even daily exercise didn't eliminate the conditions. Tom did not have a weight problem, but did have a belly. This diet got his immune system to rebuilding all his body joints. Nature heals if you give it a chance.

Yes, it is possible to be skinny and of normal weight – and still have a belly that needs processing by correct diet and lifestyle.

By latest count, Tom has lost 25 pounds in three months.

He's given the diet information to his sister back east, and she's now going on the diet.

Harry (pizza shop owner – an occupational hazard) . . . He's stopped eating his pizzas, and has reached his goal by going on the diet and is overjoyed with his new waist measurement.

He's promised me the biggest and best pizza he makes.

Too bad, I can't accept the offer!

A Heart and Cancer Patient — My dental nurse's mother was tired and felt weak constantly. She'd had heart surgery and a pacemaker implanted. And as a result of another checkup was diagnosed with colon cancer and was told she would need surgery and chemotherapy as a follow-up.

She had the surgery but refused to take the chemotherapy. Instead she went on the Do It Naturally Food Plan and did everything a hundred percent. After four months the doctor's diagnosis was that she was now free of cancer. And did not need the chemotherapy!

You can imagine the relief now felt by her and her family. They have written this testimonial to substantiate all the facts, including the above incidents.

This information has now put a new spin on my priorities, which were originally a weight loss program. We now have a documented statement of a patient who corrected both colon cancer and heart condition. This patient is now able to go back to work, lost ten pounds.

Body Types

Everyone is different – small, medium and large. We all come from various locations, and we are all used to a different home life, and exercise and eating patterns that were the norm when we were brought up. We can understand why everybody would have a different reaction undertaking this diet.

Research on sugar has shown that it can be addictive, and some people have withdrawal symptoms. However, with plenty of fruit on this diet, the sweet tooth is satisfied.

When we are young we seek out sweets as a reward, and it's regarded as a pleasure. Cake at a birthday party is traditional, and of course soda to wash it down.

So many people have to psyche themselves up before they are ready to start this diet, but after one week, they are not only losing weight, but belly size is down and they feel better. They now realize that this works. They now have motivation to continue until they reach their goal.

There are those big boned people who require more food to keep them going, and this is the way it should be.

There is the heavy construction worker, who puts in a hard day's work, and is constantly moving, lifting, hammering, shoveling, etc. These people also require appropriate food intake for the energy spent.

Then there is the office worker who sits at a desk all day, goes home and sits all evening watching TV. It is apparent that this individual will need an entirely different food intake than the construction worker. It is also apparent, that such an individual needs to add exercise to their lifestyle.

There are those who do a combination of both mental and physical work. Artists, dancers, etc. They too require individual diets and intake of food.

Each of these groups have their own individual requirements. Our instinctive hunger signals and emotional triggers will determine the results.

General Eating Guidelines

Don't eat fatty foods.

Don't eat any foods you don't like.

Don't eat any foods that disagree with you.

Don't eat foods you are allergic to.

Don't eat foods just because it's given to you, like at a party or at work.

Don't eat food combinations that disturb your body.

Don't eat questionable food- if you have any doubt of its source, age content, who handled it, etc.

Don't drink liquids with your meals. Fluids taken with your meal can dilute the hormones in your digestive fluids.

Don't over eat.

Eat melons by themselves.

Why Watermelon?

Even though watermelon is considered a fruit, it is really a vegetable. Watermelon has been certified by the American Heart Association because of its health properties and meets all nutritional requirements for health benefits.

Lycopene is the red pigment found in watermelon and is a healthy antioxidant. There are over 1,200 varieties world-wide. The US and Mexico use just 50 varieties. Watermelon is available year round. The highest producer in the world is China.

In the US, the highest producer is Florida. They are hardy plants and easy to grow and very rich in vitamins and minerals.

Long distance marathon runners, on their journey, have stations where chunks of watermelon are picked up and stuffed in their mouths while running. They tell me this is the most wonderful boost to their energy, as well as quenching their thirst. Watermelon is one of the most nutritious, enjoyable and satisfying foods to eat. And no side effect (are you listening, Ephedra users?). In China, watermelon is eaten at all meals and is a staple.

The Reason I Say "No" To Bread

We have been led to believe that bread was the staff of life. Perhaps this may have been true at a time in history when pure, healthful bread was produced. Today, what they have done to wheat is a crime against humanity. Every step from seed to final result has turned it into a chemically loaded product with only empty calories.

Bread has contributed to many serious problems including obesity, diabetes, etc. People are misled to believe this is a healthful food. The marketing and advertising people have done their job to sell us a bill of goods, when in fact bread is a contributing cause of several diseases including celiac disease. When the whole kernel of wheat is grown food processing removes the wheat germ, the endosperm, bran and wheat germ oil. What is left is the white flour, which is used to make all bakery products. Like bread, cake, cookies, crackers, pasta, etc.

Because all the valuable parts of the whole kernel of wheat have been removed, all that remains are the empty calories. The reason food processors remove these ingredients is the need for long shelf life, low cost; for wheat to be profitable it can't become rancid. White flour has a very long shelf life. But think of what it's doing to our health!

A good assignment for you is to follow the manufacturing process of a typical cereal like Corn Flakes, or any other boxed cereal. Each process sequence from the raw product to the end result leaves us with empty calories. The so-called "enriched" vitamins added is really a deception that makes one think that this is good nutrition. It's loaded with empty calories and you're better off with naturally grown fruits and vegetables. The making of breakfast cereals is an insult to humanity.

The adding of enriched vitamins are really total deceptions making one believe it is wholesome. Though it may be possible to make good organic bread, I find it not possible to be assured of its purity. You can do very nicely without bread.

Milk

Many people are allergic to milk, and with good reason. Cows today are injected with substances that are commercially used to increase profits without regards to potential health hazards. Milk is pasteurized and homogenized, which fragments the natural milk and makes it less nutritious and a compromised product, which may or may not be a cause of allergies for some. There are other substitutes, like soy milk, that may be acceptable. But this too is a controversial product. More research needs to be done on soy products, as to its safety and long range effects on future use. Non-fat, dry milk is probably a good form of milk and can be used for those who can't tolerate milk.

A good hot drink "a substitute for coffee" is made with half a tsp. of pure cocoa powder and 1 cup of non-fat, dry milk (1 cup water + 1/3 cup non-fat, dry milk).

Eat Out At Your Own Risk

You must be aware that sometimes food preparers don't follow appropriate hygienic methods. Questionable methods of preparing food may not be the best. Many a food-poisoning incident has occurred. There are large portions of food served, and there is that tendency to overeat. Because you didn't buy the ingredients yourself, you are unaware of the quality and the age of the food. Many people don't want to complain when something doesn't taste right, but they eat it anyway.

Digestive problems are very often due to eating out. As a general rule, eating at home is the better way to go. It's safer and it's less expensive.

What – No Wine, Beer or Cocktails?

Even a single drink of alcohol can be enough to impair someone's ability to reason, according to a study monitoring brainwaves in volunteers given drinks. Even "modest drinks" are enough to erode the mind's ability to detect and correct errors. Reaction time, especially when driving, is impaired. Drunk driving is rampant. The death rate is shockingly high. Tragic events on our highways because of this have created "Mothers Against Drunk Drivers," an organization that has forced more strict control over this situation. Alcohol addiction can bring inestimable damage to the afflicted and their families.

As far as I'm concerned there's nothing good about consuming alcohol, and it's not friendly to your body.

What - No Pills?

Hippocrates, the world's greatest doctor, said: "In the future, food will be your medicine, and medicine will be your food."

My father lived to be 102. He never took any pill in his life – not even an aspirin. You can get along just fine on this diet because you will be eating real food. You will be getting satisfied because you have a large variety of delicious and nutritious foods in their natural state. If you feel you must have your pills, go ahead and continue taking them but, as time goes by, you can reduce the doses gradually and wean yourself away from them. After all, there's nothing natural about these man-made products.
You will feel great relief when you have the knowledge that you don't have to take another pill again. And anybody trying to sell you a bill of goods – you know what they really want out of you!

Magic Weight Loss Pill

There are no supplements, diet drinks, energy bars, medicines, costly books, smoothies, enemas or products of any kind on this program.

You may ask:
What are you selling? How do you make your money?
What's the catch?

This is a non-profit venture. That's it – pure and simple. There is no solicitation of any kind, and you may reproduce anything here.

My hope is to help those who want to achieve better health and happiness, and reach the feeling of wellbeing to which they are entitled. This program will not only allow you to live longer, but will also give you improved quality of life without degenerative ailments.

If you have been successful in your pursuit to reach your goal, be it losing weight or correcting ailments, give this book to someone who will benefit from this information.

Health is the only true wealth.

Fruits and Vegetables

Talk about convenience foods, there's nothing better than fruit. It's the kind of food nature intended us to eat. It is loaded with minerals and vitamins that our bodies crave. No preparation is necessary. No cooking or processing is needed. The tastes, (especially if organic) are unbeatable. The colors and aromas are superb. Of course, this is food easily digestible, and friendly to our digestive system. Combinations of various fruits are the components of a perfect meal, including nuts.
Satisfaction guaranteed.

Note: Certain types of fruits need to be eaten alone. Melons, citrus and sweet fruits are best eaten at separate meals.

Diabetic and hypoglycemic people need to substitute vegetables for the fruit, because of the high sugar content.

This book is in no way a criticism of any other diet. There are several diets that have worked for some people, and many are satisfied with their personal results.
But, according to statistics, a very large percentage have left their diet program and gone back to their old lifestyle. I

believe the reasons for this varies from one person to another.

There is a definite need for education regarding nutrition in our schools. Obesity in children is now in epidemic proportions. Two thirds of the nation is overweight. And it's no wonder. We are taught to eat according to the food pyramid. Note the recommendation of bread, cereal and pasta (it's all backwards).

It's no wonder that we in this country have this high rate of overweight and obese people. To alleviate this condition there is a critical need to revise our old fashioned diet ways that have caused so much harm, no matter what the implications of this change (**though the heavens fall**). Our health is our number one priority. Through word of mouth this information will spread and become part of our lives.

Psyching Yourself Up

Some people, before starting this diet, have to think about it for some time. Some wait a week or more. Eventually upon seeing the success others are having on this diet, they then are motivated to start. After a week on this diet the results are apparent, and they usually continue the diet and are very happy with the results.

Some people need additional help to get started and just can't get enough willpower to commit to this program. There is help available. Hypnotherapy works, and can do wonders to get you into the proper state of mind. Many addictions, be it smoking, alcohol, overeating, etc., can be helped even with only one session of hypnotherapy.
It is certainly worth a try if you've given up and find things hopeless.

A Better Way

Archeologists have unearthed 4500 years old mummies of grown adults. The remarkable finding was to note that all teeth in the skeleton were there. Today, even babies 1 year old have cavities. The average person today – of any age, needs dental work, gum repair, and false teeth – both upper and lower.

Well, this only points to one thing, and that's our diet. Pure and simple. A change to 100% natural diet: no sugar, no white flour, preservatives, etc... could make a big difference in your life. Try it, you'll like it, especially with all your teeth. I know of one dentist that does follow strict adherence to The Diet. He, his wife and their four children have no cavities. You can profit from this information by sticking to the diet.

Deviations

We don't have anyone that I know of who is perfect 100% of the time. After all, we are human and our cravings sometimes carry us away from our goal.

If you follow this plan, you can expect remarkable results quickly, but if you stray off you can anticipate less results than desired and slower progress.
So, because of some reason or other, you do find yourself off your program, start the next day without any guilt feelings.

Get on course again.

But remember what triggered off your misadventure – empty calories.

Was it a party, potluck, all-you-can-eat restaurant, Chinese, Italian, pizza, fast-food? Or some well-meaning friend offering a little morsel that she wants you to taste?

After a few of these episodes, you will be able to say: No Thank You.

And you are on track again, and a much stronger person. If need is indicated, a fast of either juice or water only – up to three days – will help considerably to clear things up.

It's best to have three meals a day. Some skip breakfast thinking it's better, but it's not. Your watermelon in the morning has many minerals and vitamins that are essential to your well-being and it's satisfying, not too heavy, and stays with you – especially if you are to exercise.

Drinking water helps flush your organs to eliminate toxins and helps along processing and lubrication. Detoxification is improved.

Train yourself to eat the right food in sufficient quantities, but stop before you are too full. Overeating of any food can have detrimental effects.

So good judgment in the selection of quality and quantity of food is the prime factor of success in this program.

You will be challenged daily at meal times as to what to eat, and you will be exposed to all kinds of temptations. After being on this diet a while, you will look at food in a different light, thinking, "is this stuff I really need to nourish my body?"

Testimonials #2

Jennifer – Was the kind of woman that men die for. When she walked into a room, everyone stopped and stared at her beauty. The men would eyeball her and could not keep their eyes away and the women they were with knew that they didn't have a chance to compare with this kind of beauty. She had the high cheekbones of Katherine Hepburn, a hint of Mona Lisa's smile, the neck of Audrey Hepburn, and a figure to die for.

Her heritage was Spanish, German and Italian. For some reason I can't understand, she took a shine to me and always wanted to dance with me. And when we danced it was an experience, the kind one very rarely has. It's as close to heaven as one can get, that dancers dream about. Jennifer, who worked out regularly, had a firm, muscular body yet a feminine appearance. She was very agile because of her gymnastic and Flamenco dance experience.

She had a Masters degree, spoke several languages including German, Russian, Spanish, Italian and Chinese (she was a French teacher). An extremely intelligent, well-read individual. She was financially secure, owning many properties, expensive automobiles and prestigious homes. She was 49, looked half her age... **And felt life had passed her by.**

Now, Jennifer had a poor self-image, thought she looked ugly and nothing would convince her otherwise. You would think that such a person, who had all that going for her, would be happy. She felt miserable, didn't feel well and, after learning what her diet consisted of I knew why! Breakfast consisted of three doughnuts and coffee, a croissant and two candy bars. Cookies on the run and fast foods of all descriptions make a very dysfunctional Jennifer. Jennifer was taking medicines for depression, anxiety, anger management, as well as sleeping pills. And other vitamins and supplements which apparently weren't working.

I convinced her to try my food plan for one week and she agreed. She said she was going to the store that very evening and getting a watermelon. During the test week of this new food plan, she threw away all her doughnuts, cookies, chocolate and candy bars in the trash can.

She stated to me that, for the first time, she had lost a heaviness and felt full of energy and alive. When we danced again, I did notice an improved capability and endurance she had acquired.

She told me she will stay on this food plan from now on. And I had saved her life!

Amy…My most enthusiastic fan was Amy. She was a waitress at Denny's. My brother and I eat there for brunch frequently and we have become very well acquainted with Amy. She is the fastest waitress you have ever seen and is well liked by all because she gives good service, by practically running from kitchen to customer.

She's an attractive, normal built blond of average height and weight. And you would think she didn't need to lose weight. But after reading my book, she went on the

Program. In three weeks she lost eleven pounds. Her skin cleared up and she felt great. She gave up her coffee and other "unmentionables." She had been wanting to lose this weight for years and now she was only four pounds away from her goal. There's no question of her reaching it. She said, "why didn't someone tell me about this 30 years ago?" "Now," she said, "I'm getting my husband on the diet."

Seymour – Seymour is a naturopathic doctor, works out regularly, eats a healthy vegetarian diet and looks the picture of health. Seymour didn't show up in the gym for a couple of weeks, and when he did I sensed something was wrong. His face didn't look right, and he is 41. I asked, "what happened?" Oral surgery requiring a total anesthetic and the removal of most of his teeth. A very painful experience requiring stitches and a very high cost had taken place.

I could not understand why someone so experienced in nutrition would have such a need for this extensive operation. Seymour explained that he was brought up on junk food throughout his childhood and it wasn't until he was 13 years old that he realized what was going on. By then it was too late, the damage had been done. All his teeth were rotten and no amount of dentistry would repair the damage that had taken place in his youth. Who do we blame for this tragedy? The parents, food processors, sugar manufacturers, advertising companies or ignorance? Any and all of these people are to blame. Isn't it about time we educate the public. How many Seymour's will have to go through this ordeal? Seymour is now enlightened by my diet.

George — My brother George is four years older than me, and though he never drove a car, he gets around pretty well by walking many miles every day. He is a good example of the benefits of walking. He also has a stationary bike and a rowing machine and works it daily. He's coming around to the Food Plan and has cut down dramatically on his sugar and flour foods with a noticeably fit figure and loss of weight.

He's been a big help promoting the book and has done much public relations work in this regard. He is a prolific writer and a volunteer at the Remington Club, a nursing home and Senior resident facility. He has been awarded Volunteer of the Year for his dedication and time. George has been volunteering his time and expertise as a professional listener, where he lets those who need to talk to someone of their problems. This is a great relief to those who want to get it off their chest. I am proud of the guy and the wonderful work he is doing for his fellow man. He is my right hand man. I believe when you do unselfish good to the people, like George does, the reward, though not monetary, is far more significant.

Tom – He's a good friend of mine. In fact we are both the same age, went to the same schools when we were kids in New York City, and by coincidence met in the gym. We share many memories of the good ol' days. Tom has had a successful business career, is retired and enjoys the good life. He has the best that money can buy. The only thing he's wanting in, and unable to get, is his health.

You see, he likes to go out to the best restaurants for his gourmet foods and does so frequently. The result is a belly that won't go down and heavy weight that is playing havoc on his joints. There is constant need to doctor his symptoms. In vain, I tried to convince him to change his food intake to no avail.

Being set in his ways, the habits are too difficult to change. But when pain became too much for him to bear, he came around and finally got the message. Today, after trashing all those foods that contributed to his state of health, he completely changed his food plan and has taken the pledge "no more bagels!"

Better late then never. He's on the Program now. The belly is going down. The pain is going down. I believe he's learned his lesson the hard way and won't go back anymore.

Chapter 2

Supporting Factors

A Higher Power

Whether you're a believer, agnostic, or atheist you can't escape the wonders of the body. This is the most wonderful machine that is self-repairing with systems that are far more complex than anything made by man. Each cell is itself a complete organism. And there are trillions of them.

The organization of electrical and mechanical components, and its central control system to the brain, is a marvel that man is studying and continually learning in order to improve our lives. And there is a lot we don't know.

It is interesting that biblical laws, if obeyed, would promote good health and combat disease. It is stated many dietary laws still apply. The commands make a distinction between clean and unclean foods. References to eating fruit from the trees and the vine, and food from the earth.

55

They tell us these are not only ancient laws, but they apply today. The higher power is trying to tell us something. Don't you think we should listen?

Let's go back to our Garden of Eden. Live like nature intended.

Nutritionally good food is what we need to demand of the producers of our vegetables, fruits, poultry, fish and all other foods. Let's put the Life Force back into our food. We need to eliminate all additives and chemicals that are destroying our lives.

Religion's Ally, Gluttony

One of the chief drawing cards in our houses of worship is the after service "Breaking of Bread." Each church or synagogue has their own type of Fellowship program. You may find all kinds of food there. Including Krispy Kreme doughnuts, cookies, pie, spaghetti, fried chicken, potluck pastries, devil's food cake, candy, sodas, bagels, ice cream, brownies, etc. Often there's a big birthday cake or wedding cake and lots of coffee to wash it all down with!

All organizations in general have been geared toward food. Particularly junk food. Food has become our culture's false God.

It is up to those in this part of society to redirect this attachment of food and educate those leaders how to break this addiction to food. We will have to preach self-control.

I propose all leaders be given guidelines to follow in order to combat the obesity epidemic. My book, *No Sugar, No Flour Will Give ME the Power* can be such a guideline.

We must take whatever means to stop this steadily climbing trend to obesity. We must change the eating habits of our country. Future generations depend on us.

Economics

When shopping at the supermarket, note all the items you don't buy anymore. Look and see what others buy. Not only is this cost-effective, but you are buying the healthiest food available without any of those items that are empty calories. You will find shopping easy and fast.

Fruits and vegetables are tops on your list. There are several sources besides supermarkets like organic food stores and farmer markets.

Shopping this way will simplify your life, because you'll have eliminated many nonessentials, and substituted real nourishing and delicious food.

Of course, you'll have to do some food preparation at home. But it pays off.

Let's Be Reasonable

First the good news. You, who have followed the diet, know by now the benefits of keeping up the good work. You have been rewarded with not only weight loss, but a sense of well-being. You are not about to blow it on some sweet morsel. Everyone is different so we can expect some people find it harder to make the transition.

You must consider all the TV and newspaper advertisements touting those foods that you know don't belong in your diet . . . . and it's hard to change. You will find while on this diet your need for food will be diminished in comparison to what it was before. Not to worry. This is what it's all about. You can get by with less food, and be healthier, and live longer.

Price Pottinger, a prestigious research foundation located in San Diego, California, conducted a study with cats. They had a control group which was fed 50% less than the others. This group lived substantially longer than the other cats, who were fed their normal amount of food.

You are going to reach your goal and stay that way.

What I Eat

1. Watermelon for breakfast

2. For lunch . . . mixed raw salad of lettuce, tomatoes, cucumber, jicama, avocado, radish, and hardboiled egg . . . or . . . sardines, tuna, salmon, beef stew, chicken soup, chicken, baked potato, bean dish with vegetable and meat.

3. For dinner . . . mixed fresh fruit, or mixed raw vegetable salad, applesauce, compote or tapioca.

For snacks (when hungry) . . . fruit, nuts, compote, tapioca, celery, carrot sticks, applesauce. If going out to a restaurant, I ask for substitutes. You'll be pleasantly surprised at your options. If going to a pizza place, I scrape off the topping to eat and throw away the crust. If going for a hamburger or hot dog place I throw away the bun!

What's happening to our food?

I went into my local supermarket to buy some unsweetened coconut flakes where I had purchased them previously. The only kind available was the sweetened ones. In inquiring, the management told me they have discontinued the unsweetened coconut because the sweetened ones have longer shelf life. This makes it better and cost-effective for them. But does it make it better for us?

With obesity and overweight problems at epidemic proportions, don't you think it's about time we call the shots about sugar in our food and its relationship to the overweight problems, but also the effects sugar has on our chemical balance, and the degenerative diseases incurred?

Grow Your Own Organic Garden

One of life's biggest tragedies is not having your own garden and producing your own food. I know everyone can't have a garden, but those who can don't take advantage of the opportunity to do so.

If you only knew the advantages I'm sure you'd consider this undertaking. Because you can control the soil applying only natural composted material there would be no need for pesticides and chemical sprays. The tastes are outstanding.

Healthy food = Healthy bodies.

Dental problems diminish. Economic windfall. It's easier than you think.

Think of the seeds we discard. We can replant these seeds and with propagation and grafting teach those who want to learn how to grow their food by themselves. Hunger can be eliminated. If we have the capability of sending a man to the moon, I'm certain we can harness our brainpower and we can implement this system.

Then there are the homeless who can work gardens for food. There could be an abundance of food supply for everyone and improved health.

Compost

It's not really that complicated to understand that what we take out of the ground, returns to the ground, and naturally decomposes into a black mass. This is the fertilizer, or food, for the tree or the plant. This is nature's way of perpetuating our food supply.

The present method of disposing "garbage" at home in the garbage disposal and landfill – what a waste.

There are several ways to make compost: the container compost that revolves, the plain pile layered, the pit buried underground, and the covered organic material with soil.

Get into the habit of filling a bowl with all the fruit and vegetable peelings, eggshells and any other organic material to produce compost. It's simple, cost effective, and environmentally correct.

The fruit from fruit trees grown in this medium is far superior in taste, and has healthy minerals and vitamins, which are better than chemically treated soils. You only have to taste the difference and you'll know.

Recommendations

Even though this book promotes a weight-reduction diet, it is more than that. It is a way of life. It's a return to the world that was when food and soil were pure.

Uncovering the great deception, and extinguishing once and for all those profit motivated that have bled our people dry with their concoctions of evil is needed. Our youth and vigor have been stolen from our lives using modern marketing skills.

The advertising industry has successfully sold us a bill of goods. We need new leadership with unselfish motives. These people will be knowledgeable about the facts needed to reach the goal of our new dawn. We will no longer ignore those historians who have provided us with valuable data that show us how to live.

Over the centuries we have drifted away from the honest way of good health to one of unbalanced body chemistry. It is always best to know the truth. Large myths build up by piling myth upon myth. The result: important facts are hidden from the people, they are tricked into the propaganda with dire results.

Chapter 3

Health

Our Greatest Challenge Today
Smaller Meals

Let's face it, we are a nation of overeaters. It's no wonder that we have reached the point of being the fattest nation in the world. We just eat too much food and the results are the obesity epidemic we are in.

Just look at typical menus at restaurants. We begin by having bread and butter (while waiting to be served the food). Then there is the soda, beer, wine or cocktails. Then the appetizer, salad, soup, entrée and, of course, the dessert, washed down with coffee.

And now that's just too much food. It's enough to feed a whole family in a small village. What got us into this situation is the "more is better" philosophy – and the bigger the portions the more pleased we were (as we were getting our money's worth). Competitive practices induced the restaurants to increase the size of the food portions in order to entice more customers into their business.

Unfortunately we have followed this pattern into the home. The results of these indiscretions are now very apparent and we are in an obesity epidemic. I'm also worried about the children, as they are following their role models - their parents. The challenge is to change their eating habits.

Of course, there are other factors in this challenge that cause obesity.

1 – Stress

2 - Processed Food Manufacturers

3 – Beverage Manufacturers

4 – Advertising Media

5 – Government Guidelines

6 – Genetics

So we have a tough job ahead of us in order to get to a rational way of eating. We must inform those needing this information and show them how to get on a stable lifestyle and gradually change the eating habits of our nation.

This will take a lot of work and time. But it will pay off in the long run. There are so many people who suffer from this disease and have given up hope that they would ever recover. They can now see the light at the end of the tunnel.

I believe we are all entitled to a feeling of well-being. Following a program to reach this goal should be free for everyone who needs this information. We will need cooperation from both government and private sector.

NUTRITION LABEL FACTS:
(Grams vs. Teaspoons)
All Nutrition labels are in METRIC.
Don't you think our labels should be in a system that we understand? And SUGAR Should be Listed in BOLD!
Not many people would understand the significance of the harmful ingredients listed that lead to the degenerative diseases of today.

12 oz

WORST KEPT SECRET!

4 grams = 1 teaspoon

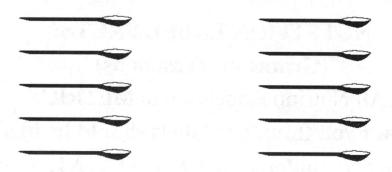

10 tsp. of sugar in every can of soda.
40g of Sugar = 10tsp of Sugar

Overwhelming evidence has shown that
excess sugar is hazardous to our health.Artificial
sweeteners themselves have caused neurological disorders

and other problems. It's best to avoid artificial sweeteners and the health issues they can bring.

What The Doctors Say

My Dentist said: "If only people would watch their diet and avoid sugar, then dental problems would be substantially reduced."

My Podiatrist said: "I see a lot of fat people. It's my opinion that if they lost weight, there would be less foot problems."

My Cardiologist said: "This diet is the best I've seen to achieve success and reach a healthy goal."

An Orthopedic Doctor said: "For every 10 lb. Loss of body weight, you will relieve your knees of 60 lbs.

Why We Have Obese Children

Looking over a recent issue of *Women's Day* magazine recently I noticed the usual subjects that mothers and housewives are interested in; recipes, herbal remedies, weight loss ideas, etc. But what impressed me the most was the advertisements aimed at mothers, suggesting what foods to get for their families:

Kelloggs Smart Start Soy Protein (corn flakes)
Starburst Jellybeans
Nestle Toll House Candy Bars
Snickers
Gevalia Kaffe coffees
Murray Sugar Free Cookies
Triscuit Crackers with Jam
Hidden Valley Ranch Dressing
Lunchables
Fruity & Cocoa Pebbles
Pasta Dish
Kraft Macaroni
McCormick Vanilla for Pie, Cake & Cookies
Pillsbury Pie Crusts & Cherry Filling
Birthday Cake
Chocolate Truffle Pie
Brownie Sundae Fudge Sauce
Lemon Meringue Bars
Welch's Fruit Snacks
Oscar Meyer Ham Sandwich
Cookie Haven
Refrigerator Jam
Chocolate Dipped Coconut Macaroons

The advertisements imply that these are all good, healthy, acceptable foods, so attractively displayed that one is lead to believe that they too would enjoy eating this.

Now let's get down to the facts. The ads are very costly. Therefore much thought goes into investing many thousands of dollars in an ad. The decisions are determined after many surveys and research of the eating habits of our country.

The food process industry knows full well what will turn people on to a product. They constantly introduce new products that will build up the curiosity of the people so they therefore feel they must try and sample it.

When I sec overweight school children eating all the junk food, I realize that they are doomed to become obese adults like their parents with every health problem, including diabetes, heart problems, Autism, attention deficit disorders, cancer, etc.

The humiliation that obese children endure is pitiful. They are left out of many social events. Their endurance is impaired, depression is rampant and they feel it's a hopeless situation. And some attempt suicide.

Some are fortunate and with psychological help can overcome this and get back to normal weight. Wouldn't it be wonderful if we can nip it in the bud and start children on a sensible food plan right from the start? They would not have to grow up in the miserable body of an obese person.

So just revising the same ingredients in a new named product usually results in a sales windfall and everyone is happy . . . except those who eventually suffer the consequences of their diet debauchery.

Entire families are so duped into this game – and of course you know what kind of results you can expect. You will be safe if you follow the *No Sugar No Flour Diet*.

Who's Happy?

I asked a child, what is happiness? The reply was, "The Smiling Face." But it is not as simple as that. The dictionary defines happiness as a state of well-being and contentment. We see a lot of smiling faces around us, but happiness is an entirely different story, made up of many factors; like good fortune, prosperity, joy, pleasurable satisfaction, and more. In order to achieve this goal, one must first of all be fit, with a positive attitude.

In meeting numbers of people, and questioning them about their health, I encountered an amazing number of complaints that bother them: tiredness, headaches, heartburn, arthritis, diabetes, memory loss, hip and knee replacement, digestive problems, constipation, high blood pressure, weakness, obesity and several rare diseases. Not to mention colds, tooth decay, eye and ear problems, prostate, and of course The Big C, cancer. The list goes on and on.

They Are All Diet Related Diseases!

Now what would be the most logical procedure to alleviate, and hopefully eliminate, these conditions? I propose that in order to do this, a new attitude must be implemented beginning with discarding all objectionable foods – don't give it away to someone, trash it!

Begin The Plan as outlined in this book, making sure you only consume the best quality you can get. You will be amazed at the difference in how you feel, the energy and strength, and, of course, a feeling of well being.

As each person is different, the time to reach your goal will vary. But you will reach your goal! **Then you will know true happiness.**

Fat Man in the Store

I was in a stationery store. A very obese man in front of me dropped his credit card. He tried to pick it up but because of his huge belly he couldn't do it. I picked it up for him, and told him I could help him if he wished. I found out that he had several things wrong; diabetes, emphysema (he was on oxygen) and arthritis was hurting his knees (the weight didn't help his knees). He wanted to have a bariatic bypass operation but the doctors refused as his diabetes made him too much of a risk.

He convinced me he would try this program for 1 week. His comment was "Do I have to give up cookies?" The man was short and weighted 315lbs. His goal was to go down to 200lbs.

I think he'll make it! Every one wants to survive.

Stress

It's inevitable, we all live with some kind of stress. Nothing ever goes 100% smoothly. And there are the little things: traffic, parking, waiting in long lines, car trouble, laundry, house-cleaning, disagreeable-inconsiderate people, high-level noise, loneliness, loss of loved ones and friends, deadlines to meet, disappointments, clutter, and finances…the list goes on and on.

It's inevitable, we all have to endure all kinds of stress in our lives. Sometimes it's overwhelming. How we cope with this depends a lot on our mental and physical condition.

If you have been diligent in this Food Program, your attitude will be positive. And you will be better able to handle life's stress better than if you had been lax. In the meantime, you will find that all of life's stress will be like "water off a duck's back."

This is a tribute to you who have maintained this program, and brought your health up to where it's entitled to be.

Colds

Colds take a heavy toll on us. Every year billions of dollars are lost. Let alone the misery and agonizing discomfort of all the symptoms. There seems to be nothing that can stop this onslaught once you get it. Doctors tell us antibiotics do not stop it. Millions of dollars are spent on over-the-counter medications. Research has proven them worthless and sometimes harmful, with side effects.

The general consensus is that no matter what you do to

remedy the situation it will take a couple of weeks to overcome…if you're lucky. Invariably colds linger on and sometimes develop into a more serious stage, like flu, pneumonia, or bronchitis, which can result in death.

Thank God there is the doctor who will take care of you in an emergency! Doctors do the best they know how to alleviate the condition. But when it comes down to it, you've got to ride it out. This is the first year of my life that I can remember going through a whole year without a cold! Do you think the Food Plan and lifestyle I've adapted had anything to do with it? This story needs to be told.

Research on the common cold costs hundreds of millions of dollars and all the work is to find a pill to cure this minor affliction. It's no longer considered minor. We now have SARS…the deadly virus that's killing hundreds all over the world.

The search for a vaccine goes on, the pharmaceutical companies say they are close to a cure. But this research is a total flop and as of this date there is no effective vaccine or treatment known. And it kills a large percentage of those infected, the costs in human life, the misery. The economies of entire nations are struck down. Severe Acute Respiratory Syndrome (SARS) goes on.

When are they going to realize, there is no magic pill? They keep doing the same old cold research all over again…money down the drain, and no hope for the afflicted is in sight. Every year we look forward to getting our cold, flu or pneumonia shot, which either works or doesn't! They tell us this is the only insurance we know that will help us to keep colds from invading our body. The following season they tell us there's a new virus around.

How We "Catch" a Cold

The general belief is contact from another person, through coughs, sneezing, or spray of virus in the air entering the nose infecting the sinus and moving into the lungs and blood stream. Apparently this theory though it seems plausible, is not the answer at all.

I wonder if we are ready for a new approach to dispel the old "scientific method" being used. Lets get down to the truth of the matter. We "catch" a cold when our bodies are vulnerable and open to any virus that's going around. Our immune system is in such a state, and its effectiveness to work properly simply cannot protect us. If our immune system worked properly and was in a healthy condition, nature protects us from any invading "virus."

The only way we can have a healthy immune system is through a healthy lifestyle including diet and exercise. This is the kind of research we should be doing. Don't you think it's about time we begin such a program?

The Immune System

Your immune system protects you from invasion of foreign bacteria and substances that are not friendly to the body.

When in a healthy condition it functions the way it should, and does its job. However when it is unreasonably overloaded, it doesn't function the way it was intended. The way to a healthy immune system is a healthy food plan and lifestyle. The rewards are significant.

There is much research that still needs to be done in this area. There are many unknown functions of the immune system and in time the mysteries will be unfolded. You can anticipate that the so called "incurable diseases" of today will be a thing of the past. I shall be looking forward to the future researchers who will make lives functioning the way they should, without the degenerative diseases of today. And we will know how to live, and how to reach our full potential we are entitled to. We will have the life span and longevity one can never imagine today! There is much education to be done and there is a new awareness that is slowly taking place. Changes in lifestyle to better ones are becoming apparent. I feel positive the near future will bring about this new world.

What's New With Diabetes?

The American Diabetes Association recently started a new campaign to promote education to stem the epidemic of diabetes in our country.

The program is called "small steps." It endorses exercise and diet. For the life of me, I couldn't detect a single thing different than what was proposed 40 years ago. If we are going to lick this thing, we will have to get the real experts, and get their actual research. These people will tell you what must be eliminated from our diets.

There may be industries that may have to substitute

other products. But that is a small price to pay when a nations present and future health is concerned. What will happen to the obese kids 20 years from now?

Listen to Your Body

In addition to the five senses (sound, sight, smell, taste and feeling) we have other senses that give us signals that tell us that we need to attend to a specific condition.

Ignoring these signals is a sure sign of trouble that sometimes ends in death. You would be surprised to learn how many prominent people from all walks of life have died because they have neglected to pay attention to nature's voice.

In our modern world, we have lost a precious instinct of survival or it has become jaded.

Our priorities are just senseless. We abuse ourselves in so many ways. Material things take on more importance than our health. **Health is the only true wealth.**

If you have been feeling ill, or hurting anywhere, do not ignore it. It is your body's signal telling you something is wrong. See your practitioner. A simple diagnosis and identification of the problem can ease your mind and, if caught in time, can save your life.

Animals Appetites Vary

Animals, like people, are different from one another. I have three cats – ages 18, 15, and 7. It is interesting to notice the behavior patterns of each of these magnificent creatures.

Amber — age 18, is a female. She has always been trim, perfectly healthy, never needing a vet for anything. She eats sparingly, and is discriminating of what she eats. And her dishes must be clean before she will eat or drink. Jones — age 15, is a male. He is overweight, and a big overeater. I try not to give him too much food, but he gets it from other places with the resulting big belly. Otherwise, he's in good health.

Redcat — age 7, is a male. He's a real chowhound, and eats like a horse. But he is in good shape. Must have a good metabolism. He is active and healthy.

The three cats are indoor/outdoor, and eat only dry and canned cat food. They are affectionate and a joy to have.

They sleep a lot, and then they are active.

I believe we can learn a lot about lifestyles from cats. They come in different sizes, and in different appetites.

Our Primitive Ancestors

Our ancestors were better nourished than we are. They ate principally of the fruits of the trees, and produce of the garden. Eventually they became hunters, and ate their food fresh. Food was eaten whole, not processed and refined, adulterated, chemically-preserved, and conditioned. They were not sprayed with poisonous insecticides, not artificially-colored and flavored, as food manufacturers do. Then, man's own instincts guided him in living, but he has forgotten how to interpret that language, and is now unable to use it as a reliable guide.

Prehistoric man fasted when he was ill or injured. Today, we are told "Eat to keep up your strength," and other scientific theories. This is counter productive to recovery.

Primitive man was much stronger than man today.

Doctors

People often neglect to go to their doctors when they are not feeling well. This is not a wise thing to do because nature has given you a sign that something is wrong. Many a person has died because of this neglect. Doctors have studied and have had practice with many patients and they know better because of their vast experience and knowledge of the anatomy and physiology as well as in their practice. You would be surprised to learn of the many people who have not heeded the call of pain when they should have gone to a doctor. These are some of the reasons why people don't go to a doctor.

"I don't want to know about it."

"It will get better by itself"

"I know better than the doctor"

"I haven't got the time"

"I'm afraid to take those terrible tests"

"I hate shots"

"I'll do it next week"

"I don't have the money"

Here is what happens when you don't go to the doctor when you should.

It doesn't get better.

The pain increases.

The condition that was minor is now major.

Psychologically you are upset.

They waited too long.

You can see how important it is to go to your doctor when you need to.

Pills: Adverse Reactions or Side Effects

Every year many new medications are introduced, and many medications are removed from the market. The reasons are very obvious, some medications have proven to be ineffective; with anti-productive side effects causing painful complications and even death. Unfortunately research sometimes was faulted with the results being disastrous.

The medication is removed from the market and a new "improved" item is introduced. All these medications are marketed with the anticipation of windfall profits. This comes at high costs.

Have you ever read the summary that drug companies place with the advertisement for their drugs? The part with the tiny, tiny print, that points out the possible adverse reactions to the drug. Because of this warning, it takes the liability off the drug company. This legal maneuver removes the blame for any mishap occurring off their shoulders. You now share the responsibility of your health with the practicing physician who prescribed the medication.

It is best to read the small print in the summary before you take any medication. Unfortunately adverse reactions do sometimes occur. Many deaths that are due to adverse reactions are recorded, but a great many of the deaths are not reported as to the proper cause, "adverse reaction."

Even doctors and their families suffer from medical mishaps. Traditional medicine causes a percentage of premature deaths. This includes nursing shortages, overworked and inexperienced staff, plus human errors. Some doctors are leaving the profession because malpractice suits are causing them to go into bankruptcy.

Always read the small print in the summary before you take a medication, after all you are entitled to know the risks before you put anything in your mouth or body. You have the choice to go this route, or Do It Naturally!

Ronald Reagan: President or Pauper

It puzzles me how a man like President Ronald Reagan, who held the most important position in our country, with the respect of all peoples of the world, could be a victim of Alzheimer Disease. He had the capability and power to accomplish tasks that would change the world, and he did. He led our country through one of our most trying times.

It puzzles me that with all the latest technology, advanced medical breakthroughs, his regular physical examinations by the finest doctors, and the staff of people taking extraordinary measures to protect this person that they could not do a thing to help him stop the suffering of Alzheimer's Disease, which he had for 10 years and finally died.

What a waste – He was an extraordinary individual with natural talents in many areas. Besides political know-how and acting abilities, he was a great communicator. And yet his golden years that could have been so productive were denied him.

The popular theory of Alzheimer's Disease is that there is no known cause, and no cure. I know differently; it's a diet-related disease. The information is out there. All one has to do is ask.

What is more debilitating than processed sugar or artificial sweeteners? President Reagan was never without his colorful jellybeans; in his Oval Office, at home, or on vacations, always near by. It was a kind of funny, identifiable whimsy. No one ever dreamed that they could possibly be dangerous during those days. Today's illuminating scientific studies prove the error of his habits. The ingestion of these harmful substances (sugar, and artificial sweeteners & flavors- none natural) cause serious health problems such as diabetes, cancer, and various emotional disorders. Every mother knows what sugar does to a child.

Education, tons of it, has got to be implemented. In our homes and schools. Sermons by our religious leaders of all faiths could help in this effort, by making people aware of adapting a healthy lifestyle.

Just think, if President Reagan had this vital information available, his last 10 years (or more) could have been productive and enjoyable. Think of all the grief that Nancy and family would have avoided. Yet his golden years, which could have been so productive, were denied him.

There Can't Be a Cure Until You Remove the Cause!

The American Indians of 1492

Of the many tribes, the Choctaw, lived a life that is far advanced as a civilization we could learn from. They were a healthy people, noted for their strength and endurance.

The mothers about to deliver their babies in a few hours, delivered the baby alone without the help of any midwife. It was painless, and they then resumed their occupations. This is a degree of health rarely observed in civilized women. They grew fruit, vegetables, and nuts. Their hunting was strictly for food, never sports. Corn was their staple article of food. They also had beans, potatoes, pumpkins, and honey. Most of their food was eaten raw with minimum preparation. No one owned land, and food was equally divided by all. They were active people engaged in sports, they wore little clothes. The gold-hungry Europeans did considerable harm by their ruthlessness. We owe a debt to the Indians.

Chapter 4

There Is Hope

Reuters Article (As appeared in San Diego Union Tribune, 5-6-04):

Obesity Conference: Lawsuits Could Help
Washington – Lawsuits may be a good way to force food makers to produce more healthful foods or curb ads that encourage overeating, speakers at an obesity conference said yesterday.

Two-thirds of adult Americans are overweight or obese. Poor diet and inactivity is now the No. 2 cause of preventable death, killing about 400,000 Americans each year, the government says. Fifteen percent of U.S. children are overweight.

Some speakers at the annual Consumer Federation of America conference on food and nutrition said trial lawyers and state attorneys general can be helpful by filing innovative suits that prompt food makers to produce healthier foods.

Associated Press Article (As appeared in San Diego Union Tribune, 5-5-04):
School Is Junk-Food Free To Check Obesity.

NEW HAVEN, Conn. – At Nathan Hale School, candy bars are confiscated. Bake sales are frowned upon. The vending machines don't carry soda – only water, milk or juice.

This is a "junk food-free school," an early phase of a district-wide initiative to fight childhood obesity. It's where third-graders have salads if they don't like the main course, and where seventh-grade girls do exercises after school.

Nationwide, many schools are reconsidering their vending machine offerings and changing their lunchroom food lineup. But New Haven, an urban district on Connecticut's shoreline, is particularly committed.

"There isn't a candy bar in this school," says Principal Kim Johnsky as she surveys the maze of lunch tables.

Nathan Hale, a K-8 school, is the first to go completely junk-free. Next fall, all schools will get a touch of the healthy treatment as the program expands.

Vending machine choices will be overhauled: baked chips will replace fried, granola will replace cookies. Cafeterias in elementary and middle schools have already rolled out baked versions of things like chicken nuggets and french fries, and fried foods will be gradually phased out of high schools, too.

The district has started cooking classes for parents and infuses regular science classes with nutrition lessons. Building renovations include designs for larger gyms to encourage physical activity.

Even the bake sale, a traditional source of fund-raising for classes and parent organizations, is being discouraged in favor of plant sales and penny drives.

In New Haven, the poverty rate is so high the system has a universal free lunch program. The district doesn't have hard data on how many students are obese, but officials say a significant number of its 20,400 students have diabetes.

Nationally, about 15 percent of children and adolescents between the ages 6 and 19 are obese, according to government figures.

Dr. Stephen Updegrove, a medical adviser for New Haven Schools and one of the primary architects of the district's policy, said one goal is to create a "ripple effect" from the school to community.

Chapter 5

Research

The Problem

The eating habits of people today have resulted in the present epidemic of overweight and obesity. We are constantly exposed to all kinds of media that promotes the way of life that will induce people to follow a given pattern that suggests what kind of a lifestyle to follow. Companies and corporations who are profit motivated will of course strive for higher income strategies that will induce the public to buy their products. Windfall profits is their goal. Various sales tactics are used to woo the people to buy their products.

Radio, television, newspapers and magazines are some of the methods used in advertising their wares. This pays off and the profits roll in. Now there's nothing wrong with making money . . . legitimately. However, not when it results in harming and killing people. Society today accepts the way we eat and drink as it is done today.

The Solution

Education will be the answer to our overweight and obesity problem. We will need to use those tactics that have been successful such as in the smoking epidemic. People have been made aware of its devastating harm and now regulations prohibit its use in various establishments today. It will take time and dedicated unselfish individuals to get this program to reach a successful goal. There again we will have to use the same types of media and of course the schools will teach the new programs that result in the lifestyle change we are striving for. There will always be people who will disagree with any change in their life.

Once we see that this program works, and people are happy with their feeling of well being, improved health…there will be a snowball effect when they see for themselves others that have gone this way of life and reached their goal. There will be a new positive attitude in our country.

"124 Ways Sugar Can Ruin Your Health"
NANCY APPLETON PhD.

Contributed by Nancy Appleton, Ph.D., "http://www.nancyappleton.com"www.nancyappleton.com Author of *Lick The Sugar Habit*.

In addition to throwing off the body's homeostasis, excess sugar may result in a number of other significant consequences. The following is a listing of some of sugar's metabolic consequences from a variety of medical journals and other scientific publications.

1. *Sugar can suppress the immune system*
2. *Sugar upsets the mineral relationships in the body*
3. *Sugar can cause hyperactivity, anxiety, difficulty concentrating, and crankiness in children*
4. *Sugar can produce a significant rise in triglycerides*
4. *Sugar contributes to the reduction in defense against bacterial infection (infectious diseases)*
5. *Sugar causes a loss of tissue elasticity and function, t he more sugar you eat the more elasticity and function you lose*
6. *Sugar reduces high density lipoproteins*
7. *Sugar leads to chromium deficiency*
8. *Sugar leads to cancer of the breast, ovaries, prostrate,*

and rectum

9. *Sugar can increase fasting levels of glucose*
10. *Sugar causes copper deficiency*
11. *Sugar interferes with absorption of calcium and magnesium*
12. *Sugar can weaken eyesight*
13. *Sugar raises the level of neurotransmitters: dopamine, serotonin, and norepinephrine*
14. *Sugar can cause hypoglycemia*
15. *Sugar can produce an acidic digestive tract*
16. *Sugar can cause a rapid rise of adrenaline levels in children*
17. *Sugar malabsorption is frequent in patients with functional bowel disease*
18. *Sugar can cause premature aging*
19. *Sugar can lead to alcoholism*
20. *Sugar can cause tooth decay*
21. *Sugar contributes to obesity*
22. *High intake of sugar increases the risk of Crohn's disease, and ulcerative colitis*
24. *Sugar can cause changes frequently found in person with gastric or duodenal ulcers*
25. *Sugar can cause arthritis*
26. *Sugar can cause asthma*
27. *Sugar greatly assists the uncontrolled growth of Candida Albicans (yeast infections)*

28. *Sugar can cause gallstones*
29. *Sugar can cause heart disease*
30. *Sugar can cause appendicitis*
31. *Sugar can cause multiple sclerosis*
32. *Sugar can cause hemorrhoids*
33. *Sugar can cause varicose veins*
34. *Sugar can elevate glucose and insulin responses in oral contraceptive users*
35. *Sugar can lead to periodontal disease*
36. *Sugar can contribute to osteoporosis*
37. *Sugar contributes to saliva acidity*
38. *Sugar can cause a decrease in insulin sensitivity*
39. *Sugar can lower the amount of Vitamin E in the blood*
40. *Sugar can decrease growth hormone*
41. *Sugar can increase cholesterol*
42. *Sugar can increase the systolic blood pressure*
43. *Sugar can cause drowsiness and decreased activity in children*
44. *High sugar intake increases advanced glycation end products (AGEs)(Sugar bound non- enzymatically to protein)*
45. *Sugar can interfere with the absorption of protein*
46. *Sugar causes food allergies*
47. *Sugar can contribute to diabetes*
48. *Sugar can cause toxemia during pregnancy*
49. *Sugar can contribute to eczema in children*

50. Sugar can cause cardiovascular disease
51. Sugar can impair the structure of DNA
52. Sugar can change the structure of protein
53. Sugar can make our skin age by changing the structure of collagen
54. Sugar can cause cataracts
55. Sugar can cause emphysema
56. Sugar can cause atherosclerosis
57. Sugar can promote an elevation of low density lipoproteins (LDL)
58. High sugar intake can impair the physiological homeostasis of many systems in the body
59. Sugar lowers the enzymes ability to function
60. Sugar intake is higher in people with Parkinson's disease
61. Sugar can cause a permanent altering the way the proteins act in the body
62. Sugar can increase the size of the liver by making the liver cells divide
63. Sugar can increase the amount of liver fat
64. Sugar can increase kidney size and produce pathological changes in the kidney
65. Sugar can damage the pancreas
66. Sugar can increase the body's fluid retention
67. Sugar is enemy #1 of the bowel movement
68. Sugar can cause myopia (nearsightedness)

69. Sugar can compromise the lining of the capillaries
70. Sugar can make the tendons more brittle
71. Sugar can cause headaches, including migraines
72. Sugar plays a role in pancreatic cancer in women
73. Sugar can adversely affect school children's grades and cause learning disorders
74. Sugar can cause an increase in delta, alpha, and theta brain waves
75. Sugar can cause depression
76. Sugar increases the risk of gastric cancer
77. Sugar can cause dyspepsia (indigestion)
78. Sugar can increase your risk of getting gout
79. Sugar can increase the levels of glucose in an oral glucose tolerance test over the ingestion of complex carbohydrates
80. Sugar can increase the insulin responses in humans consuming high-sugar diets compared to low sugar diets
81. High refined sugar diet reduces learning capacity
82. Sugar can cause less effective functioning of two blood proteins, albumin, and lipoproteins, which may reduce the body's ability to handle fat and cholesterol
83. Sugar can contribute to Alzheimer's disease
85. Sugar can cause platelet adhesiveness
86. Sugar can cause hormonal imbalance; some hormones become underactive and others become overactive

87. Sugar can lead to the formation of kidney stones
88. Sugar can lead the hypothalamus to become highly sensitive to a large variety of stimuli
89. Sugar can lead to dizziness
90. Diets high in sugar can cause free radicals and oxidative stress
91. High sucrose diets of subjects with peripheral vascular disease significantly increases platelet adhesion
92. High sugar diet can lead to biliary tract cancer
93. Sugar feeds cancer
94. High sugar consumption of pregnant adolescents is associated with a twofold increased risk for delivering a small-for-gestational-age (SGA) infant
95. High sugar consumption can lead to substantial decrease in gestation duration among adolescents
96. Sugar slows food's travel time through the gastrointestinal tract
97. Sugar increases the concentration of bile acids in stools and bacterial enzymes in the colon
98. Sugar increases estradiol (the most potent form of naturally occurring estrogen) in men
99. Sugar combines and destroys phosphatase, an enzyme, which makes the process of digestion more dificult
100. Sugar can be a risk factor of gallbladder cancer
101. Sugar is an addictive substance

102. Sugar can be intoxicating, similar to alcohol

103. Sugar can exacerbate PMS

104. Sugar given to premature babies can affect the amount of carbon dioxide they produce

105. Decrease in sugar intake can increase emotional stability

106. The body changes sugar into 2 to 5 times more fat in the bloodstream than it does starch

107. The rapid absorption of sugar promotes excessive food intake in obese subjects

108. Sugar can worsen the symptoms of children with attention deficit hyperactivity disorder (ADHD)

109. Sugar adversely affects urinary electrolyte composition

110. Sugar can slow down the ability of the adrenal glands to function

111. Sugar has the potential of inducing abnormal metabolic processes in a normal healthy individual and to promote chronic degenerative diseases
I.Vs (intravenous feedings) of sugar water can cut off oxygen to the brain

112. High sucrose intake could be an important risk factor in lung cancer

113. Sugar increases the risk of polio

114. High sugar intake can cause epileptic seizures

115. Sugar causes high blood pressure in obese people
116. In Intensive Care Units: Limiting sugar saves lives
117. Sugar may induce cell death
118. Sugar may impair the physiological homeostasis of many systems in living organisms
119. In juvenile rehabilitation camps, when children were put on a low sugar diet, there was a 44% drop in antisocial behavior
120. Sugar can cause gastric cancer
121. Sugar dehydrates newborns
122. Sugar can cause gum disease
123. Sugar increases the estradiol in young men
125. Sugar can cause low birth weight babies

References

Sanchez, A., et al. Role of Sugars in Human Neutrophilic Phagocytosis, American Journal of Clinical Nutrition. Nov 1973;261:1180_1184. Bernstein, J., al. Depression of Lymphocyte Transformation Following Oral Glucose Ingestion. American Journal of Clinical Nutrition.1997;30:613.

Couzy, F., et al."Nutritional Implications of the Interaction

Minerals," Progressive Food and Nutrition Science 17;1933:65-87.

Goldman, J., et al. Behavioral Effects of Sucrose on Preschool Children. Journal of Abnormal Child Psychology.1986;14(4):565_577.

Scanto, S. and Yudkin, J. The Effect of Dietary Sucrose on Blood Lipids, Serum Insulin, Platelet Adhesiveness and Body Weight in Human Volunteers, Postgraduate Medicine Journal. 1969;45:602_607.

Ringsdorf, W., Cheraskin, E. and Ramsay R. Sucrose,Neutrophilic Phagocytosis and Resistance to Disease, Dental Survey. 1976;52(12):46_48.

Cerami, A., Vlassara, H., and Brownlee, M."Glucose and Aging." Scientific American. May 1987:90. Lee, A. T. and Cerami, A. The Role of Glycation in Aging. Annals of the New York Academy of Science; 663:63-67.

Albrink, M. and Ullrich I. H. Interaction of Dietary Sucrose and Fiber on Serum Lipids in Healthy Young Men Fed High Carbohydrate Diets. American Journal of Clinical Nutrition. 1986;43:419-428. Pamplona, R., et al. Mechanisms of Glycation in Atherogenesis. Med Hypotheses. Mar 1993;40(3):174-81.

Kozlovsky, A., et al. Effects of Diets High in Simple Sugars on Urinary Chromium Losses. Metabolism. June 1986;35:515_518.

Takahashi, E., Tohoku University School of Medicine,

Wholistic Health Digest. October 1982:41:00

Kelsay, J., et al. Diets High in Glucose or Sucrose and Young Women. American Journal of Clinical Nutrition. 1974;27:926_936. Thomas, B. J., et al. Relation of Habitual Diet to Fasting Plasma Insulin Concentration and the Insulin Response to Oral Glucose, Human Nutrition Clinical Nutrition. 1983; 36C(1):49_51.

Fields, M.., et al. Effect of Copper Deficiency on Metabolism and Mortality in Rats Fed Sucrose or Starch Diets, Journal of Clinical Nutrition. 1983;113:1335_1345.

Lemann, J. Evidence that Glucose Ingestion Inhibits Net Renal Tubular Reabsorption of Calcium and Magnesium. Journal Of Clinical Nutrition. 1976 ;70:236_245.

Acta Ophthalmologica Scandinavica. Mar 2002;48;25. Taub, H. Ed. Sugar Weakens Eyesight, VM NEWSLETTER;May 1986:06:00

Sugar, White Flour Withdrawal Produces Chemical Response. The Addiction Letter .Jul 1992:04:00

Dufty, William. Sugar Blues. (New York:Warner Books, 1975).

Ibid.

Jones, T. W., et al. Enhanced Adrenomedullary Response and Increased Susceptibility to Neuroglygopenia: Mechanisms Underlying the Adverse Effect of Sugar Ingestion in Children. Journal of Pediatrics. Feb 1995;126:171-7.

Ibid.

Lee, A. T.and Cerami A. The Role of Glycation in Aging. Annals of the New York Academy of Science.1992;663:63-70.

Abrahamson, E. and Peget, A.. Body, Mind and Sugar. (New York:Avon,1977.}

Glinsmann, W., Irausquin, H., and Youngmee, K. Evaluation of Health Aspects of Sugar Contained in Carbohydrate Sweeteners. F. D. A. Report of Sugars Task Force. 1986:39:00 Makinen K.K.,et al. A Descriptive Report of the Effects of a 16_month Xylitol Chewing_gum Programme Subsequent to a 40_month Sucrose Gum Programme. Caries Research. 1998; 32(2)107_12.

Keen, H., et al. Nutrient Intake, Adiposity, and Diabetes. British Medical Journal. 1989; 1:00 655_658

Persson P. G., Ahlbom, A., and Hellers, G. Epidemiology. 1992;3:47-52.

Yudkin, J. New York: Sweet and Dangerous.:Bantam Books:1974: 129

Darlington, L., Ramsey, N. W. and Mansfield, J. R. Placebo_Controlled, Blind Study of Dietary Manipulation Therapy in Rheumatoid Arthritis, Lancet. Feb 1986;8475(1):236_238.

Powers, L. Sensitivity: You React to What You Eat. Los Angeles Times. (Feb. 12, 1985). Cheng, J., et al. Preliminary Clinical Study on the Correlation Between

Allergic Rhinitis and Food Factors. Lin Chuang Er Bi Yan Hou Ke Za Zhi Aug 2002;16(8):393-396.

Crook, W. J. The Yeast Connection. (TN:Professional Books, 1984)..

Heaton, K. The Sweet Road to Gallstones. British Medical Journal. Apr 14, 1984; 288:00:00 1103_1104. Misciagna, G., et al. American Journal of Clinical Nutrition. 1999;69:120-126.

Yudkin, J. Sugar Consumption and Myocardial Infarction. Lancet..Feb 6, 1971:1(7693):296-297. Suadicani, P., et al. Adverse Effects of Risk of Ishaemic Heart Disease of Adding Sugar to Hot Beverages in Hypertensives Using Diuretics. Blood Pressure. Mar 1996;5(2):91-71.

Cleave, T. The Saccharine Disease. (New Canaan, CT: Keats Publishing, 1974).

Erlander, S. The Cause and Cure of Multiple Sclerosis, The Disease to End Disease." Mar 3, 1979;1(3):59_63.

Cleave, T. The Saccharine Disease. (New Canaan, CT: Keats Publishing, 1974.)

Cleave, T. and Campbell, G. (Bristol, England:Diabetes, Coronary Thrombosis and the Saccharine Disease: John Wrightand Sons, 1960).

Behall, K. Influ ence of Estrogen Content of Oral Contraceptives and Consumption of Sucrose on Blood Parameters. Disease Abstracts International. 1982;431437.

Glinsmann, W., Irausquin, H., and K. Youngmee.

Evaluation of Health Aspects of Sugar Contained in Carbohydrate Sweeteners. F. D. A. Report of Sugars Task Force.1986;39:36_38.

Tjäderhane, L. and Larmas, M. A High Sucrose Diet Decreases the Mechanical Strength of Bones in Growing Rats. Journal of Nutrition. 1998:128:1807_1810.

Appleton, N. New York: Healthy Bones. Avery Penguin Putnam:1989.

Beck_Nielsen H., Pedersen O., and Schwartz S. Effects of Diet on the Cellular Insulin Binding and the Insulin Sensitivity in Young Healthy Subjects. Diabetes. 1978;15:289_296 .

Journal of Clinical Endocrinology and Metabolism. Aug 2000

Gardner, L. and Reiser, S. Effects of Dietary Carbohydrate on Fasting Levels of Human Growth Hormone and Cortisol. Proceedings of the Society for Experimental Biology and Medicine. 1982;169:36_40.

Reiser, S. Effects of Dietary Sugars on Metabolic Risk Factors Associated with Heart Disease. Nutritional Health. 1985;203_216.

Hodges, R., and Rebello, T. Carbohydrates and Blood Pressure. Annals of Internal Medicine. 1983:98:838_841.

Behar, D., et al. Sugar Challenge Testing with Children Considered Behaviorally Sugar Reactive. Nutritional Behavior. 1984;1:277_288.

Furth, A. and Harding, J. Why Sugar Is Bad For You. New Scientist. Sep 23, 1989;44.

Simmons, J. Is The Sand of Time Sugar? LONGEVITY. June 1990:00:00 49_53.

Appleton, N. New York: LICK THE SUGAR HABIT. Avery Penguin Putnam:1988. allergies

Sucrose Induces Diabetes in Cat. Federal Protocol. 1974;6(97). diabetes

Cleave, T.:The Saccharine Disease: (New Canaan Ct: Keats Publishing, Inc., 1974).131.

Ibid. 132

Vaccaro O., Ruth, K. J. and Stamler J. Relationship of Postload Plasma Glucose to Mortality with 19_yr Follow_up. Diabetes Care. Oct 15,1992;10:328_334.

Tominaga, M., et al, Impaired Glucose Tolerance Is a Risk Factor for Cardiovascular Disease, but Not Fasting Glucose. Diabetes Care. 1999:2(6):920-924.

Lee, A. T. and Cerami, A. Modifications of Proteins and Nucleic Acids by Reducing Sugars: Possible Role in Aging. Handbook of the Biology of Aging. (New York: Academic Press, 1990.).

Monnier, V. M. Nonenzymatic Glycosylation, the Maillard Reaction and the Aging Process. Journal of Gerontology 1990:45(4):105_110.

Dyer, D. G., et al. Accumulation of Maillard Reaction Products in Skin Collagen in Diabetes and Aging. Journal of Clinical Investigation. 1993:93(6):421_22.

Veromann, S.et al."Dietary Sugar and Salt Represent Real Risk Factors for Cataract Development." Ophthalmologica. 2003 Jul-Aug;217(4):302-307.

Monnier, V. M. Nonenzymatic Glycosylation, the Maillard Reaction and the Aging Process. Journal of Gerontology. 1990:45(4):105_110.

Pamplona, R., et al. Mechanisms of Glycation in Atherogenesis. Medical Hypotheses . 1990:00:00 174_181.

Lewis, G. F. and Steiner, G. Acute Effects of Insulin in the Control of Vldl Production in Humans. Implications for Theinsulin-resistant State. Diabetes Care. 1996 Apr;19(4):390-3 R. Pamplona, M. .J., et al. Mechanisms of Glycation in Atherogenesis. Medical Hypotheses. 1990;40:174-181.

Ceriello, A. Oxidative Stress and Glycemic Regulation. Metabolism. Feb 2000;49(2 Suppl 1):27-29.

Appleton, Nancy. New York; Lick the Sugar Habit. Avery Penguin Putnam, 1988 enzymes

Hellenbrand, W. Diet and Parkinson's Disease. A Possible Role for the Past Intake of Specific Nutrients. Results from a Self-administered Food-frequency Questionnaire in a Case-control Study. Neurology. Sep 1996;47(3):644-650. 61 Cerami, A., Vlassara, H., and Brownlee, M. Glucose and Aging. Scientific American. May 1987:00:00 90

Goulart, F. S. Are You Sugar Smart? American Fitness.

March_April 1991:00:00 34_38.

Ibid.

Yudkin, J., Kang, S. and Bruckdorfer, K. Effects of High Dietary Sugar. British Journal of Medicine. Nov 22, 1980;1396.

Goulart, F. S. Are You Sugar Smart? American Fitness. March_April 1991:00:00 34_38. Milwakuee, WI,: damage pancreas

Ibid. fluid retention

Ibid. bowel movement

Ibid. nearsightedness

Ibid. compromise the lining of the capillaries

Nash, J. Health Contenders. Essence. Jan 1992; 23:00 79_81.

Grand, E. Food Allergies and Migraine.Lancet. 1979:1:955_959.

Michaud, D. Dietary Sugar, Glycemic Load, and Pancreatic Cancer Risk in a Prospective Study. J Natl Cancer Inst. Sep 4, 2002 ;94(17):1293-300.

Schauss, A. Diet, Crime and Delinquency. (Berkley Ca; Parker House, 1981.)

Christensen, L. The Role of Caffeine and Sugar in Depression. Nutrition Report. Mar 1991;9(3):17-24.

Ibid.

Cornee, J., et al. A Case-control Study of Gastric Cancer and Nutritional Factors in Marseille, France, European

Journal of Epidemiology. 1995;11:55-65.

Yudkin, J. Sweet and Dangerous.(New York:Bantam Books,1974) 129

Ibid, 44

Reiser, S., et al. Effects of Sugars on Indices on Glucose Tolerance in Humans. American Journal of Clinical Nutrition. 1986:43;151-159.

Reiser,S., et al. Effects of Sugars on Indices on Glucose Tolerance in Humans. American Journal of Clinical Nutrition. 1986;43:151-159.

Molteni, R, et al. A High-fat, Refined Sugar Diet Reduces Hippocampal Brain-derived Neurotrophic Factor, Neuronal Plasticity, and Learning. NeuroScience. 2002;112(4):803-814.

Monnier, V., Nonenzymatic Glycosylation, the Maillard Reaction and the Aging Process. Journal of Gerontology. 1990;45:105-111.

Frey, J. Is There Sugar in the Alzheimer's Disease? Annales De Biologie Clinique. 2001; 59 (3):253-257.

Yudkin, J. Metabolic Changes Induced by Sugar in Relation to Coronary Heart Disease and Diabetes. Nutrition and Health. 1987;5(1-2):5-8.

Ibid.

Blacklock, N. J., Sucrose and Idiopathic Renal Stone. Nutrition and Health. 1987;5(1-2):9- Curhan, G., et al. Beverage Use and Risk for Kidney Stones in Women.

Annals of Internal Medicine. 1998:28:534-340.

Journal of Advanced Medicine. 1994;7(1):51-58.

Ibid

Ceriello, A. Oxidative Stress and Glycemic Regulation. Metabolism. Feb 2000;49(2 Suppl 1):27-29.

Postgraduate Medicine.Sept 1969:45:602-07.

Moerman, C. J., et al. Dietary Sugar Intake in the Etiology of Biliary Tract Cancer. International Journal of Epidemiology . Ap 1993;.2(2):207-214.

Quillin, Patrick, Cancer's Sweet Tooth, Nutrition Science News. Ap 2000 Rothkopf, M.. Nutrition. July/Aug 1990;6(4).

Lenders, C. M. Gestational Age and Infant Size at Birth Are Associated with Dietary Intake among Pregnant Adolescents. Journal of Nutrition. Jun 1997;1113- 1117

Ibid.

Bostick, R. M., et al. Sugar, Meat.and Fat Intake and Non-dietary Risk Factors for Colon Cancer Incidence in Iowa Women. Cancer Causes & Control. 1994:05:00 :38-53.

Ibid. Kruis, W., et al. Effects of Diets Low and High in Refined Sugars on Gut Transit, Bile Acid Metabolism and Bacterial Fermentation. Gut. 1991;32:367-370. Ludwig, D. S., et al. High Glycemic Index Foods, Overeating, And Obesity. Pediatrics. Mar 1999;103(3):26-32.

Yudkin, J and Eisa, O. Dietary Sucrose and Oestradiol Concentration in Young Men. Annals of Nutrition and

Metabolism. 1988:32(2):53-55.

Lee, A. T. and Cerami A. The Role of Glycation in Aging. Annals of the New York Academy of Science. 1992; 663:63-70.

Moerman, C., et al."Dietary Sugar Intake in the Etiology of Biliary Tract Cancer." International Journal of Epidemiology. Ap 1993; 22(2):207-214.

Sugar, White Flour Withdrawal Produces Chemical Response. The Addiction Letter. Jul 1992:04:00

Colantuoni, C., et al. Evidence That Intermittent, Excessive Sugar Intake Causes Endogenous Opioid Dependence. Obes Res. Jun 2002 ;10(6):478-488. Annual Meeting of the American Psychological Society, Toronto, June 17, 2001 HYPERLINK "/2001/june/30/sugar.htm"www.mercola,com/2001/june/30/sugar.htm

Ibid.

The Edell Health Letter. Sept 1991;7:1.

Sunehag, A. L., et al. Gluconeogenesis in Very Low Birth Weight Infants Receiving Total Parenteral Nutrition Diabetes. 1999 ;48 7991_800.

Christensen L., et al. Impact of A Dietary Change on Emotional Distress. Journal of Abnormal Psychology .1985;94(4):565_79.

Nutrition Health Review. Fall 85 changes sugar into fat faster than fat

Ludwig, D. S., et al. High Glycemic Index Foods, Overeating and Obesity. Pediatrics. March 1999;103(3):26-32.

Pediatrics Research. 1995;38(4):539-542. Berdonces, J. L. Attention Deficit and Infantile Hyperactivity. Rev Enferm. Jan 2001;4(1)11-4

Blacklock, N. J. Sucrose and Idiopathic Renal Stone. Nutrition Health. 1987;5(1 & 2):9-17.

Lechin, F., et al. Effects of an Oral Glucose Load on Plasma Neurotransmitters in Humans. Neurophychobiology. 1992;26(1-2):4-11.

Fields, M. Journal of the American College of Nutrition. Aug 1998;17(4):317_321.

Arieff, A. I. Veterans Administration Medical Center in San Francisco. San Jose Mercury; June 12/86. IVs of sugar water can cut off oxygen to the brain.

De Stefani, E."Dietary Sugar and Lung Cancer: a Case_control Study in Uruguay." Nutrition and Cancer. 1998;31(2):132_7.

Sandler, Benjamin P. Diet Prevents Polio. Milwakuee, WI,:The Lee Foundation for for Nutritional Research, 1951

Murphy, Patricia. The Role of Sugar in Epileptic Seizures. Townsend Letter for Doctors and Patients. May, 2001 Murphy Is Editor of Epilepsy Wellness Newsletter, 1462 West 5th Ave., Eugene, Oregon 97402

Stern, N. & Tuck, M. Pathogenesis of Hypertension in

Diabetes Mellitus. Diabetes Mellitus, a Fundamental and Clinical Test. 2nd Edition, (PhiladelphiA; A:Lippincott Williams & Wilkins, 2000)943-957.

Christansen, D. Critical Care: Sugar Limit Saves Lives. Science News. June 30, 2001; 159:404.

Donnini, D. et al. Glucose May Induce Cell Death through a Free Radical-mediated Mechanism.Biochem Biohhys Res Commun. Feb 15, 1996:219(2):412-417.

Ceriello, A. Oxicative Stress and Glycemic Regulation. Metabolism. Feb 2000;49(Suppl I):27-29.

Schoenthaler, S. The Los Angeles Probation Department Diet-Behavior Program: Am Empirical Analysis of Six Institutional Settings. Int J Biosocial Res 5(2):88-89.

Cornee, J., et al. A Case-control Study of Gastric Cancer and Nutritional Factors in Marseille, France. European Journal of Epidemiology 11 (1995):55-65.

Gluconeogenesis in Very Low Birth Weight Infants Receiving Total Parenteral Nutrition. Diabetes. 1999

Apr;48(4):791-800.

Glinsmann, W., et al. Evaluation of Health Aspects of Sugar Contained in Carbohydrate Sweeteners." FDA Report of Sugars Task Force -1986 39 123 Yudkin, J. and Eisa, O. Dietary Sucrose and Oestradiol Concentration in Young Men. Annals of Nutrition and Metabolism. 1988;32(2):53-5.

Lenders, C. M. Gestational Age and Infant Size at Birth Are Associated with Dietary Intake Among Pregnant Adolescents. Journal of Nutrition 128 (1998):1807-181

Wheaty Indiscretions:
What Happens to Wheat From Seed to Storage
Jen Allbritton, Certified Nutritionist

Wheat — America's grain of choice. It's hardy, glutenous consistency makes it practical for a variety of foodstuffs — cakes, breads, pastas, cookies, bagels, pretzels and cereals that have been puffed, shredded and shaped. This ancient grain can actually be very nutritious when it is grown and prepared in the appropriate manner. Unfortunately, the indiscretions inflicted by our modern farming techniques and milling practices have dramatically reduced the quality of the commercial wheat berry and the flour it makes. You might think, "Wheat is wheat — what can they do that makes commercial varieties so bad?" Listen up, because you are in for a surprise!

It was the cultivation of grains — members of the grass family — that made civilization possible.Since wheat is one of the oldest known grains, its cultivation is as old as civilization itself. Some accounts suggest that mankind has used this wholesome food since 10,000 to 15,000 years BC.2 Upon opening Egyptian tombs archeologists discovered large earthenware jars full of wheat to "sustain" the Pharaohs in the afterlife. Hippocrates, the father of medicine, was said to recommend stone-ground flour for its beneficial effects on the digestive tract. Once humans figured out how to grind wheat, they discovered that when water is added it can be naturally fermented and turned into beer and expandable dough. Botanists have identified almost 30,000 varieties of wheat, which are assigned to one of several classifications according to their planting schedule and nutrient composition[3] — hard red winter, hard red spring, soft red winter, durum, hard white and soft white. Spring wheat is planted in the spring and winter wheat is planted in the fall and shoots up the next spring to mature that summer. Soft, hard, and durum (even harder) wheats are classified according to the strength of their kernel. This strength is a function of the protein-to-starch ratio in the endosperm (the starchy middle layer of the seed). Hard wheats contain less starch, leaving a stronger protein matrix.

With the advent of modern farming, the number of varieties of wheat in common use has been drastically reduced. Today, just a few varieties account for 90 percent of the wheat grown in the world.[1]

When grown in well-nourished, fertile soil, whole wheat is rich in vitamin E and B complex, many minerals, including calcium and iron, as well as omega-3 fatty acids. Proper growing and milling methods are necessary to preserve these nutrients and prevent rancidity. Unfortunately, due to the indiscretions inflicted by contemporary farming and processing on modern wheat, many people have become intolerant or even allergic to this nourishing grain. These indiscretions include depletion of the soil through the use of chemical fertilizers, pesticides and other chemicals, high-heat milling, refining and improper preparation, such as extrusion.

Rather than focus on soil fertility and careful selection of seed to produce varieties tailored to a particular micro-climate, modern farming practices use high-tech methods to deal with pests and disease, leading to over dependence on chemicals and other substances.

It Starts with the Seed

Even before they are planted in the ground, wheat seeds receive an application of fungicides and insecticides. Fungicides are used to control diseases of seeds and seedlings; insecticides are used to control insect pests, killing them as they feed on the seed or emerging seedling. Seed companies often use mixtures of different seed-treatment fungicides or insecticides to control a broader spectrum of seed pests.

Pesticides and Fertilizers

Some of the main chemicals (insecticides, herbicides and fungicides) used on commercial wheat crops are disulfoton (Di-syston), methyl parathion, chlorpyrifos, dimethoate, diamba and glyphosate.

Although all these chemicals are approved for use and

considered safe, consumers are wise to reduce their exposure as much as possible. Besides contributing to the overall toxic load in our bodies, these chemicals increase our susceptibility to neurotoxic diseases as well as to conditions like cancer.

Many of these pesticides function as xenoestrogens, foreign estrogen that can reap havoc with our hormone balance and may be a contributing factor to a number of health conditions. For example, researchers speculate these estrogen-mimicking chemicals are one of the contributing factors to boys and girls entering puberty at earlier and earlier ages. They have also been linked to abnormalities and hormone-related cancers including fibrocystic breast disease, breast cancer and endometriosis.

Hormones on Wheat?
Sounds strange, but farmers apply hormone-like substances or "plant growth regulators" that affect wheat characteristics, such as time of germination and strength of stalk. These hormones are either "natural," that is extracted from other plants, or synthetic. Cycocel is a synthetic hormone that is commonly applied to wheat.
Moreover, research is being conducted on how to manipulate the naturally occurring hormones in wheat and other grains to achieve "desirable" changes, such as

regulated germination and an increased ability to survive in cold weather.

No studies exist that isolate the health risks of eating hormone-manipulated wheat or varieties that have been exposed to hormone application. However, there is substantial evidence about the dangers of increasing our intake of hormone-like substances.

Chemicals Used in Storage

Chemical offenses don't stop after the growing process. The long storage of grains makes them vulnerable to a number of critters. Before commercial grain is even stored, the collection bins are sprayed with insecticide, inside and out. More chemicals are added while the bin is filled. These so-called "protectants" are then added to the upper surface of the grain as well as four inches deep into the grain to protect against damage from moths and other insects entering from the top of the bin. The list of various chemicals used includes chlorpyrifos-methyl, diatomaceous earth, bacillus thuringiensis, cy-fluthrin, malathion and pyrethrins.

Then there is the threshold test. If there is one live insect per quart of sample, fumigation is initiated. The goal of fumigation is to "maintain a toxic concentration of gas long enough to kill the target pest population." The toxic chemicals penetrate the entire storage facility as well as the grains being treated. Two of the fumigants used include methyl bromide and phosphine-producing materials, such as magnesium phosphide or aluminum phosphide.

Grain Drying

Heat damage is a serious problem that results from the artificial drying of damp grain at high temperatures. Overheating causes denaturing of the protein 26 and can also partially cook the protein, ruining the flour's baking properties and nutritional value. According to Ed Lysenko, who tests grain by baking it into bread for the Canadian Grain Commission's grain research laboratory, wheat can be dried without damage by using re-circulating batch dryers, which keep the wheat moving during drying. He suggests an optimal drying temperature of 60 degrees Celsius (140 degrees Fahrenheit). Unfortunately, grain processors do not always take these precautions.

Modern Processing

The damage inflicted on wheat does not end with cultivation and storage, but continues into milling and processing. A grain kernel is comprised of three layers: the bran, the germ and the endosperm. The bran is the outside layer where most of the fiber exists. The germ is the inside layer where many nutrients and essential fatty acids are found. The endosperm is the starchy middle layer. The high nutrient density associated with grains exists only when these three are intact. The term whole grain refers to the grain before it has been milled into flour. It was not until the late nineteenth century that white bread, biscuits, and cakes made from white flour and sugars became mainstays in the diets of industrialized nations and these products were only made possible with the invention of high-speed milling machines. Dr. Price observed the unmistakable consequences of these dietary changes during his travels and documented their corresponding health effects. These changes not only resulted in tooth decay, but problems with fertility, mental health and disease progression.

Flour was originally produced by grinding grains between large stones. The final product, 100 percent stone-ground whole-wheat flour, contained everything that was in the grain, including the germ, fiber, starch and a wide variety of vitamins and minerals. Without refrigeration or chemical preservatives, fresh stone-ground flour spoils quickly. After wheat has been ground, natural wheat-germ oil becomes rancid at about the same rate that milk becomes sour, so refrigeration of whole grain breads and flours is necessary. Technology's answer to these issues has been to apply faster, hotter and more aggressive processing.

Since grinding stones are not fast enough for mass-production, the industry uses high-speed, steel roller mills that eject the germ and the bran. Much of this "waste product" — the most nutritious part of the grain — is sold as "by-products" for animals. The resulting white flour contains only a fraction of the nutrients of the original grain. Even whole wheat flour is compromised during the modern milling process. High-speed mills reach 400 degrees Fahrenheit, and this heat destroys vital nutrients and creates rancidity in the bran and the germ. Vitamin E in the germ is destroyed — a real tragedy because whole wheat used to be our most readily available source of vitamin E.

Literally dozens of dough conditioners and preservatives go into modern bread, as well as toxic ingredients like partially hydrogenated vegetable oils and soy flour. Soy flour — loaded with anti-nutrients — is added to virtually all brand-name breads today to improve rise and prevent sticking. The extrusion process, used to make cold breakfast cereals and puffed grains, adds insult to injury with high temperatures and high pressures that create additional toxic components and further destroy nutrients — even the synthetic vitamins that are added to replace the ones destroyed by refinement and milling.

People have become accustomed to the mass-produced, gooey, devitalized, and nutritionally deficient breads and baked goods and have little recollection of how real bread should taste. Chemical preservatives allow bread to be shipped long distances and to remain on the shelf for many days without spoiling and without refrigeration.

Healthy Whole Wheat Products

Ideally, one should buy whole wheat berries and grind them fresh to make homemade breads and other baked goods. Buy whole wheat berries that are grown organically or biodynamically — biodynamic farming involves higher standards than organic. Since these forms of farming do not allow synthetic, carcinogenic chemicals and fertilizers, purchasing organic or biodynamic wheat assures that you are getting the cleanest, most nutritious food possible. It also automatically eliminates the possibility of irradiation31 and genetically engineered seed. The second best option is to buy organic 100 percent stone-ground whole-wheat flour at a natural food store. Slow-speed, steel hammer-mills are often used instead of stones, and flours made in this way can list "stone-ground" on the label. This method is equivalent to the stone-ground process and produces a product that is equally nutritious. Any process that renders the entire grain into usable flour without exposing it to high heat is acceptable.

If you do not make your own bread, there are ready-made alternatives available. Look for organic sourdough or sprouted breads freshly baked or in the freezer compartment of your market or health food store. If bread is made entirely with 100 percent stone-ground whole grains, it will state so on the label. When bread is stone ground and then baked, the internal temperature does not usually exceed 170 degrees, so most of the nutrients are preserved. As they contain no preservatives, both whole wheat flour and its products should be kept in the refrigerator or freezer. Stone-ground flour will keep for several months frozen. Sprouting, soaking and genuine sourdough leavening "pre-digests" grains, allowing the nutrients to be more easily assimilated and metabolized. This is an age-old approach practiced in most traditional cultures. Sprouting begins germination, which increases the enzymatic activity in foods and inactivates substances called enzyme inhibitors. These enzyme inhibitors prevent the activation of the enzymes present in the food and therefore, may hinder optimal digestion and absorption. Soaking neutralizes phytic acid, a component of plant fiber found in the bran and hulls of grains, legumes, nuts, and seeds that reduces mineral absorption. All of these benefits may explain why sprouted foods are less likely to produce allergic reactions in those who are sensitive.

Sprouting also causes a beneficial modification of various nutritional elements. According to research undertaken at the University of Minnesota, sprouting increases the total nutrient density of a food. For example, sprouted whole wheat was found to have 28 percent more thiamine (B1), 315 percent more riboflavin (B2), 66 percent more niacin

(B3), 65 percent more pantothenic acid (B5), 111 percent more biotin, 278 percent more folic acid and 300 percent more vitamin C than non-sprouted whole wheat. This phenomenon is not restricted to wheat. All grains undergo this type of quantitative and qualitative transformation. These studies also confirmed a significant increase in enzymes, which means the nutrients are easier to digest and absorb.

You have several options for preparing your wheat. You can use a sour leavening method by mixing whey, buttermilk or yogurt with freshly ground wheat or quality pre-ground wheat from the store, or soak your berries whole for 8 to 22 hours, then drain and rinse. There are some recipes that use the whole berries while they are wet, such as cracker dough ground right in the food processor. Another option is to dry sprouted wheat berries in a low-temperature oven or dehydrator, and then grind them in your grain mill and then use the flour in a variety of recipes.

Although our modern wheat suffers from a great number of indiscretions, there are steps we can take to find the quality choices that will nourish us today and for the long haul. Go out and make a difference for you and yours and turn your wheaty indiscretions into wheaty indulgences.

www.westonaprice.org/modernfood/wheatyindiscretions.html

Conflict of Interests Between Doctors and Drug Companies

From The *British Medical Journal*:
Conflict of Interests Between Doctors and Drug Companies
- The entanglement between doctors and drug companies is creating controversy in both the public and academic worlds as it becomes clear that the integrity of medical research and the prescription habits of doctors are being influenced.

The close relationship between doctors and drug companies is attracting increasing public and academic scrutiny, as drug costs grow ever higher.

Despite evidence that information from drug company representatives is often overly positive, 80 percent to 95 percent of doctors see drug reps regularly. Many doctors also receive gifts from drug companies each year.

In the United States an estimated 80,000 drug company representatives, backed by more than $19 billion of industry's combined annual promotional budgets, are visiting doctors every day.

Evidence has shown that gifts from drug companies

influence doctor's prescribing habits and have been associated with an increase in prescriptions of the promoted drug.

Forms of Drug Company Conflicts of Interest:
Face-to-face visits from drug company representatives.
Acceptance of direct gifts of equipment, travel, or accommodation.
Acceptance of indirect gifts, through sponsorship of software or travel.
Attendance at sponsored dinners and social or recreational events.
Attendance at sponsored educational events, continuing medical education, workshops, or seminars.
Attendance at sponsored scientific conferences.
Ownership of stock or equity holdings.
Conducting sponsored research.
Company funding for medical schools, academic chairs, or lecture halls.
Membership of sponsored professional societies and associations.
Advising a sponsored disease foundation or patients' group.
Involvement with or use of sponsored clinical guidelines.
Undertaking paid consultancy work for companies.
Membership of company advisory boards of "thought leaders" or "speakers' bureau"

Authoring "ghostwritten" scientific articles.

Medical journals' reliance on drug company advertising, company purchased reprints, sponsored supplements and expenses for travel or accommodation for industry-sponsored educational meetings, which often highlight the sponsor's drug, are commonly accepted by doctors. The industry has recently implemented a voluntary code to address relationships with health care professionals. However, many question the effectiveness of such codes considering that if a company flies 300 doctors to a golf resort, reimburses their costs, pays them to attend, and educates them about the company's latest drug, in order to train them to become members of the company's stable of paid speakers, the entire activity would be in compliance.

Further, many professional societies rely on industry sponsorship and their medical journals often rely on industry-funded research trials, advertisements and industry-sponsored supplements. Currently, an estimated 60 percent of biomedical research and development in the United States is privately funded.

However, there is an abundance of strong evidence that industry-sponsored research tends to yield results that are favorable to sponsor much more often than non-industry studies.

The many conflicts of interest have led one expert to say that the medical profession is being bought by the pharmaceutical industry.

Moreover, many experts agree that the entanglement between drug companies and doctors is part of the reason for ever-increasing drug costs and part of the reason why attempts to control costs are undermined.
British Medical Journal May 31, 2003;326:1189-192 (Part 1, Full Text Article)
British Medical Journal May 312003;326:1193-1196 (Part 2, Full Text Article)

Dr. Joseph Mercola's comment:

(#1 Health website on internet)

It is encouraging to see that the drug companies' far-reaching grasp is being exposed but frustrating that it has taken this long.

If you haven't seen the signs around you, please take notice. Health costs are rising through the roof, and shortly we will be spending over $2 trillion dollars a year for health care in the U.S.

It is safe to estimate that over three-fourths of this money is wasted on short-term fixes, primarily drugs and surgeries, which in no way address the long-term cause of the problem.

If those funds were redirected to optimize food and stress concerns, we would have more than enough funds left over to help the more than 40 million uninsured Americans.

Aside from the issue of compromised medical integrity that the close ties between doctors, researchers and drug companies causes, there is the major issue of regarding drugs as the solution to many medical problems — a view that is prevalent among many health care professionals.

You can give yourself the best chance of avoiding drugs altogether by boosting your body's natural defense — its immune system. You can start the process by looking into the nutrition plan and implementing an exercise program.

Unlike drugs, which often result in adverse side effects, the only side effects this method will produce are increased energy, optimized weight and emotional wellness. Plus, you'll likely save the money that would have been spent on drugs and trips to the doctor.

Related Articles:

Over Dose: The Case Against the Drug Companies

Medical Research or Drug Company Secrets?

Most Media Coverage of Drugs Highly Biased

Drug Companies Engage in Illegal Sales Practices: U.S. Issues Warning

Drug Review Process Doesn't Protect Consumers

Disclaimer - The entire contents of this website are based upon the opinions of Dr. Mercola. They are not intended to replace a one-on-one relationship with a qualified health care professional and they are not intended as medical advice. They are intended as a sharing of knowledge and information from the research and experience of Dr. Mercola and his community. Dr. Mercola encourages you to make your own health care decisions based upon your research and in partnership with a qualified health care professional.

Books for Reference

Fast Food Nation: The Dark Side of the All-American Meal by Eric Schlosser; publisher Houghton Mifflin 2001. ISBN 0-395-97789-4.

This book is a groundbreaking work of investigation and cultural history, likely to transform the way America thinks about the way it eats. If we are what we eat, then we are not well. Fast food is destroying us: individuals, communities, work and family life and indeed, our very connections with the world. Fast food is a significant part of contemporary culture and economy: in 1970, Americans spent about $6 billion on fast food; in 2000, more than $110 billion.

Americans drink soda at the annual rate of 56 gallons — or nearly 600 12-ounce cans — per capita. The book also takes up the industry's little-known practices that keep us hooked: chemicals that are added to flavor the burgers, fries, and milk shakes, to add to their attractiveness, for example, the practice of frying potatoes in fat that is 7% soy oil and 93% beef tallow.

Consumers have made the fast food industry what it is today. This book gives us — as consumers and citizens some of the tools we need to demand accountability from those in charge of its oversight and, at least partially, to reclaim our food system.

The Hungry Gene: The Science of Fat and the Future of Thin by Ellen Ruppel Shell, publisher Atlantic Monthly Press 2002. ISBN 0871138565

The Hungry Gene takes the large view of obesity. The obese constitute the largest and wealthiest drug market in the world – and Ellen Ruppel Shell is critical of drug makers rushing to develop a cure for what they have dubbed the trillion-dollar disease. Although Americans spend $33 billion a year on weight-loss products and schemes, they are fatter than ever. Fifty percent of Americans are obese, double the level of 20 years ago.

More than 9 million Americans are morbidly obese, meaning they are more than 100 pounds overweight.

The Hungry Gene draws parallels between Big Tobacco and Big Food. Shell points to evidence that foods high in fat and refined carbohydrates are addictive, highlighting recent findings that mice weaned off a fat and sugar-rich diet exhibit a state of anxiety similar to that seen in heroin withdrawal... Generally speaking, taste in food – like brand loyalty in cigarettes – is cultivated in childhood. . . So we were fooled and fooled again. This is precisely what Big Food is doing today."

Fat Land: How Americans Became the Fattest People in the World by Greg Critser, published by Houghton Mifflin 2001. ISBN 0618164723.

In *Fat Land: How Americans Became the Fattest People in the World*, reporter Greg Critser lays out the smorgasbord of cultural and economic ingredients that combine to make fatness as American as a deep-fried apple fritter. The story he tells begins in the 1970's, with Earl Butz, the Nixon agriculture secretary best known for offensive jokes.

Responding to industry and consumer pressures, Butz

loosened regulations and cut deals to bring the nation an abundance of cheap sweeteners and fats, especially high-fructose corn syrup and super-saturated palm oil. Those particularly unhealthy products made possible the huge variety of affordable, fat-and calorie-loaded convenience foods we consume today.

By the end of last century, Critser writes, "The pioneers of supersize . . . had banished the shame of gluttony and opened the maw of the American eater wider than even they had ever imagined."

In a chapter titled "What the Extra Calories Do to You," Critser ably describes the alarming health dangers of excess fat. "Today Americans are the fattest people on the face of the earth (save for the inhabitants of a few South Seas Islands)."

Our Deadly Diabetes Deception
By **Thomas Smith**, 10-18-2004
Diabetes introduction

Thomas Smith is a reluctant medical investigator, having been forced into curing his own diabetes because it was obvious that his doctor would not or could not cure it.

*He has published the results of his successful diabetes investigation in his self-help manual, **Insulin: Our Silent Killer**, written for the layperson but also widely valued by the medical practitioner. This manual details the steps required to reverse Type II diabetes and references the work being done with Type I diabetes. The book may be purchased from the author at PO Box 7685, Loveland, Colorado 80537, USA (North American residents send $US25.00; overseas residents should contact the author for payment and shipping instructions).*

Thomas Smith has also posted a great deal of useful information about diabetes on his website, *http://www.Healingmatters.com* He can be contacted by telephone at +1 (970) 669 9176 and by email at *valley@healingmatters.com*

If you are an American diabetic, your physician will never tell you that most diabetes is curable. In fact, if you even mention the cure word around him, he will likely become upset and irrational. His medical school training only allows him to respond to the word treatment. For him, the cure word does not exist. Diabetes, in its modern epidemic form, is a curable disease and has been for at least 40 years. In 2001, the most recent year for which US figures are posted, 934,550 Americans died from out of control symptoms of this disease.

Your physician will also never tell you that at one time

strokes, both ischemic and hemorrhagic, heart failure due to neuropathy as well as both ischemic and hemorrhagic coronary events, obesity, atherosclerosis, elevated blood pressure, elevated cholesterol, elevated triglycerides, impotence, retinopathy, renal failure, liver failure, polycystic ovary syndrome, elevated blood sugar, systemic candida, impaired carbohydrate metabolism, poor wound healing, impaired fat metabolism, peripheral neuropathy as well as many more of today's disgraceful epidemic disorders were once well understood to often be but symptoms of diabetes.

If you contract diabetes and depend upon orthodox medical treatment, sooner or later you will experience one or more of its symptoms as the disease rapidly worsens. It is now common practice to refer to these symptoms as if they were separable independent diseases with separate unrelated proprietary treatments provided by competing medical specialists.

It is true that many of these symptoms can and sometimes do result from other causes; however, it is also true that this fact has been used to disguise the causative role of diabetes and to justify expensive, ineffective treatments for these symptoms.

Epidemic Type II Diabetes is curable. By the time you get to the end of this article you are going to know that. You're going to know why it isn't routinely being cured. And, you're going to know how to cure it. You are also probably going to be angry at what a handful of greedy people have surreptitiously done to the entire orthodox medical community and to its trusting patients.

The Diabetes Industry

Today's diabetes industry is a massive community that has grown step by step from its dubious origins in the early twentieth century. In the last eighty years it has become enormously successful at shutting out competitive voices that attempt to point out the fraud involved in modern diabetes treatment. It has matured into a religion. And, like all religions, it depends heavily upon the faith of the believer. So successful has it become that it verges on blasphemy to suggest that, in most cases, the kindly high priest with the stethoscope draped prominently around his neck is a charlatan and a fraud. In the large majority of cases he has never cured a single case of diabetes in his entire medical career.

The financial and political influence of this medical community has almost totally subverted the original intent of our regulatory agencies. They routinely approve death dealing ineffective drugs with insufficient testing. Former commissioner of the FDA, Dr. Herbert Ley, in testimony before a US Senate hearing, commented "People think the FDA is protecting them. It isn't. What the FDA is doing and what the public thinks its doing are as different as night and day."

The financial and political influence of this medical community dominates our entire medical insurance industry. Although this is beginning to change in America, it is still difficult to find employer group medical insurance to cover effective alternative medical treatments. Orthodox coverage is standard in all states. Alternative medicine is not. For example there are only 1400 licensed naturopaths in 11 states compared to over 3.4 million orthodox licensees in 50 states.[3] Generally, only approved treatments from licensed credentialed practitioners are insurable. This, in effect, neatly creates a special kind of money that can only be spent within the orthodox medical and drug industry. No other industry in the world has been able to manage the politics of convincing people to accept so large a part of their pay in a form that does not allow them to spend it on health care as they see fit. Insurance money can only be spent within an industry that has banned the cure word from its vocabulary.

The financial and political influence of this medical community completely controls virtually every diabetes publication in the country. Many diabetes publications are subsidized by ads for diabetes supplies. No diabetes editor is going to allow the truth to be printed in his magazine. This is why the diabetic only pays about 1/4 to 1/3 of the cost of printing the magazine he depends upon for accurate information. The rest is subsidized by ads purchased by diabetes manufacturers with a vested commercial interest in preventing diabetics from curing their diabetes. When looking for a magazine that tells the truth about diabetes, look first to see if it is full of ads for diabetes supplies.

And then there are the various associations that solicit annual donations to find a cure for their proprietary disease. Every year they promise a cure is just around the corner; just send more money. Some of these very same associations have been clearly implicated in providing advice that promotes the progress of diabetes in their trusting supporters. For example, for years they heavily promoted exchange diets[4] which are in fact scientifically worthless, as anyone who has ever tried to use them quickly finds out. They have ridiculed the use of glycemic tables which are actually very helpful to the diabetic. They promoted the use of margarine as heart healthy long after it was well understood that margarine causes diabetes and promotes heart failure. Why everyone expects that these tax free associations will really self destruct by eliminating their proprietary disease and thereby destroy their only source of income is truly amazing. If people ever wake up to the cure for diabetes that has been suppressed for forty years, these associations will soon be out of business. But until then, they nonetheless continue to need our support.

For forty years medical research has consistently shown, with increasing clarity, that type II diabetes is a degenerative disease directly caused by an engineered food supply that is focused on profit instead of health. Although the diligent can readily glean this information from a wealth of medical research literature, it is generally otherwise unavailable. Certainly this information has been, and remains, largely unavailable in the medical schools that train our retail doctors.

Prominent among the causative agents in our modern diabetes epidemic are the engineered fats and oils sold in today's supermarkets.

The first step to curing diabetes is to stop believing the lie that the disease is incurable.

Diabetes History

In 1922, three Canadian Nobel prize winners, Banting, Best and Macleod, were successful in saving the life of a fourteen year old diabetic girl in Toronto General Hospital with injectable insulin. Eli Lilly was licensed to manufacture this new wonder drug and the medical community basked in the glory of a job well done.

It wasn't until 1933 that rumors about a new rogue diabetes surfaced. This was in a paper presented by Joslyn, Dublin and Marks and printed in the American Journal of Medical Sciences. This paper "Studies on Diabetes Mellitus" , discussed the emergence of a major US epidemic of a disease which looked very much like the diabetes of the early 1920s only it did not respond to the wonder drug, insulin. Even worse, sometimes insulin treatment killed the patient.

This new disease became known as Insulin Resistant Diabetes because it had the elevated blood sugar symptom of diabetes, but responded poorly to insulin therapy. Many physicians had considerable success in treatment of this disease by diet. A great deal was learned about the relationship between diet and diabetes in the 1930s and 1940s.

Diabetes, which had a per capita incidence of 0.0028% at the turn of the century, had by 1933, zoomed 1000% in the US to become a disease faced by many doctors. This disease, under a variety of aliases, was destined to go on to wreck the health of over half of the American population and to incapacitate almost 20% by the 1990s.

In 1950 the medical community became able to perform serum insulin assays. This quickly revealed that the disease wasn't classical diabetes. This new disease was characterized by sufficient, often excessive, blood insulin levels. The problem was that the insulin was ineffective; it did not reduce blood sugar. But, since the disease had been known as diabetes for almost twenty years it was renamed Type II Diabetes. This was to distinguish it from the earlier Type I Diabetes which was due to insufficient insulin production by the pancreas.

Had the dietary insights of the previous 20 years dominated the medical scene from this point and into the late 1960s, diabetes would have become widely recognized as curable instead of merely treatable. Unfortunately this didn't happen and so, in 1950, a search was launched for another wonder drug to deal with the Type II Diabetes problem.

Cure vs. Treatment

This new ideal wonder drug would be, like insulin, effective in remitting obvious adverse symptoms of the disease, but not effective in curing the underlying disease. Thus, it would be needed continually for the remaining life of the patient. It would have to be patentable; that is, it could not be a natural medication because these are non-patentable. Like insulin, it would be highly profitable to manufacture and distribute. Mandatory government approvals would be required to stimulate the use by physicians as a prescription drug. Testing required for these approvals would have to be enormously expensive to prevent other, unapproved, medications from becoming competitive.

This is the origin of the classic medical protocol of "treating the symptoms." By doing this, both the drug company and the doctor could prosper in business and the patient, while not being cured of his disease, was sometimes temporarily relieved of some of his symptoms. Additionally, natural medications that actually cured disease, would have to be suppressed. The more effective they were, the more they would need to be suppressed and their proponents jailed as quacks. After all, it wouldn't do to have some cheap effective natural medication cure disease in a capital intensive monopoly market specifically designed to treat symptoms without curing disease. Often the natural substance really did cure disease. This is why the force of law was used to drive the natural, often superior, medicines from the market place, to remove the cure word from the medical vocabulary and to totally undermine the very concept of a free marketplace in the medical business.

Now it is clear why the cure word is so vigorously suppressed by law. The FDA has extensive Orwellian regulations that prohibit the use of the cure word to describe any competing medicine or natural substance. It is precisely because many natural substances do actually both cure and prevent disease that this word has become so frightening to the drug and orthodox medical community.

The Commercial Value Of Symptoms

After this redesign of drug development policy to focus on ameliorating symptoms rather than curing disease, it became necessary to reinvent the way drugs were marketed. This was done in 1949 in the midst of a major epidemic of insulin resistant diabetes.

In 1949, the US medical community reclassified the symptoms of diabetes, along with many other disease symptoms, into diseases in their own right. With this reclassification as the new basis for diagnosis, competing medical specialty groups quickly seized upon related groups of symptoms as their own proprietary symptom set. Thus the heart specialist, endocrinologist, allergist, kidney specialist, and many others started to treat the symptoms for which they felt responsible. As the underlying cause of the disease was widely ignored, all focus on actually curing anything was completely lost. By this new focus on treating symptoms, instead of curing disease, disease was now allowed to run rampant without any effective check on its progress. While not a very smart idea from the patients viewpoint, it did succeed in making the American medical community amongst the wealthiest in the world because of the continuing high volume of repeat business that it promoted .

Heart failure for example, which had previously been understood to often be but a symptom of diabetes, now became a disease not directly connected to diabetes. It became fashionable to think that diabetes "increased cardio vascular risk." The causal role of a failed blood sugar control system in heart failure became obscured. Consistent with the new medical paradigm, none of the treatments offered by the heart specialist actually cures, or is even intended to cure, their proprietary disease. For example, the three year survival rate for bypass surgery is almost exactly the same as if no surgery was undertaken.

Today over half of the people in America suffer from one or more symptoms of this disease. In its beginnings, it has become well known to physicians as Type II Diabetes, Insulin Resistant Diabetes, Insulin Resistance, Adult Onset Diabetes, or more rarely Hyperinsulinemia. According to the American Heart Association, almost 50% of Americans suffer from one or more symptoms of this disease. One third of our population is morbidly obese. Half of our population is overweight. Type II Diabetes, also called Adult Onset Diabetes, now appears routinely in six-year-old children

Many of our degenerative diseases can be traced to a massive failure of our endocrine system that was well known to the physicians of the 1930's as Insulin Resistant Diabetes. This basic underlying disorder is known to be a derangement of the blood sugar control system by badly engineered fats and oils. It is exacerbated and complicated by the widespread lack of other essential nutrition that the body needs to cope with the metabolic consequences of these poisons.

All fats and oils are not equal. Some are healthy and beneficial; many, commonly available in the supermarket, are poisonous. The health distinction is not between saturated and unsaturated, as the fats and oils industry would have us believe. Many saturated oils and fats are highly beneficial; many unsaturated oils are highly poisonous. The important health distinction is between natural and engineered. There exists great dishonesty in advertising in the fats and oils industry. It is aimed at creating a market for cheap junk oils such as soy, cottonseed and rape seed oil. With an informed and aware public these oils would have no market at all and the US, and indeed the world, would have far less diabetes.

Epidemiological Lifestyle Link

As early as 1901, efforts had been made to manufacture and sell food products by the use of automated factory machinery because of the immense potential profits that were possible. Most of the early efforts failed because people were inherently suspicious of food that wasn't farm fresh and because the technology was poor. As long as people were prosperous, suspicious food products made little headway. Crisco, the artificial shortening, was once given away free in 2 1/2 lb cans in an unsuccessful effort to influence the US wives to trust and buy the product in preference to lard.

Margarine was introduced and was bitterly opposed by the dairy states. With the advent of the depression of the 1930s, margarine, Crisco and a host of other refined and hydrogenated products began to make significant penetration into the US food markets. Support for dairy opposition to margarine faded during WW II because there wasn't enough butter for both the civilian population and the needs of the military. At this point, the dairy industry having lost much support, simply accepted a diluted market share and concentrated on supplying the military.

Flax oils and fish oils, which were common in the stores and considered a dietary staple before the American population became diseased, have disappeared from the shelf. The last supplier of flax oil to the major distribution chains was Archer Daniel's Midland and they stopped producing and supplying the product in 1950.

More recently, one of the most important of the remaining genuinely beneficial fats was subjected to a massive media disinformation campaign that portrayed it as a saturated fat that causes heart failure. As a result, it has virtually disappeared from the supermarket shelves. Thus was coconut oil removed from the food chain and replaced with soy oil, cottonseed oil and rape seed oil.[14] Our parents would never have swapped a fine healthy oil like coconut oil for these cheap junk oils. It was shortly after this successful media blitz that the US populace lost its war on fat. For many years coconut oil had been one of our most effective dietary weight control agents.

The history of the engineered adulteration of our once clean food supply exactly parallels the rise of the epidemic of diabetes and hyperinsulinemia now sweeping the US as well as much of the rest of the world.

The second step to a cure for this disease epidemic is to stop believing the lie that our food supply is safe and nutritious.

Nature Of The Disease

Diabetes is classically diagnosed as a failure of the body to properly metabolize carbohydrates. Its defining symptom is a high blood glucose level. Type I Diabetes results from insufficient insulin production by the pancreas. Type II

Diabetes results from ineffective insulin. In both types, the blood glucose level remains elevated. Neither insufficient insulin nor ineffective insulin can limit post prandial (after eating) blood sugar to the normal range. In established cases of Type II Diabetes, these elevated blood sugar levels are often preceded by and accompanied by chronically elevated insulin levels and by serious distortions of other endocrine hormonal markers.

The ineffective insulin is no different from effective insulin. Its ineffectiveness lies in the failure of our cell population to respond to it. It is not the result of any biochemical defect in the insulin itself. Therefore, it is appropriate to note that this disease is a disease that affects almost every cell in the seventy trillion or so cells of our body. All of these cells are dependent upon the food that we eat for the raw materials that they need for self-repair and maintenance.

The classification of diabetes as a failure to metabolize carbohydrates is a traditional classification that originated in the early 19th century when little was known about metabolic diseases or about metabolic processes.[15] Today, with our increased knowledge of metabolic processes, it would appear quite appropriate to define Type 2 Diabetes more fundamentally as a failure of the body to properly metabolize fats and oils. This failure results in a loss of effectiveness of insulin and in the consequent failure to metabolize carbohydrates. Unfortunately, much medical insight into this matter, except at the research level, remains hampered by its 19th century legacy.

Thus Type II Diabetes and its early hyperinsulinemic symptoms are whole body symptoms of this basic cellular failure to properly metabolize glucose. Each cell of our body, for reasons which are becoming clearer, find themselves unable to transport glucose from the blood stream to their interior. The glucose then either remains in the blood stream, is stored as body fat or as glycogen, or is otherwise disposed of in urine.

It appears that when insulin binds to a cell membrane receptor, it initiates a complex cascade of biochemical reactions inside the cell. This causes a class of glucose transporters known as GLUT 4 molecules to leave their parking area inside the cell and travel to the inside surface of the plasma cell membrane. When in the membrane, they migrate to special areas of the membrane called caveolae areas.[16] There, by another series of biochemical reactions, they identify and hook up with glucose molecules and transport them into the interior of the cell by a process called endocytosis. Within the cells interior, this glucose is then burned as fuel by the mitochondria to produce energy to power cellular activity.

Thus these GLUT 4 transporters lower glucose in the blood stream by transporting it out of the bloodstream into all of our bodily cells.

Many of the molecules involved in these glucose and insulin mediated pathways are lipids, that is they are fatty acids. A healthy plasma cell membrane, now known to be an active player in the glucose scenario, contains a complement of cis type w=3 unsaturated fatty acids. This makes the membrane relatively fluid and slippery. When these cis fatty acids are chronically unavailable because of our diet, trans fatty acids and short and medium chain saturated fatty acids are substituted in the cell membrane. These substitutions make the cellular membrane stiffer and more sticky and inhibit the glucose transport mechanism. Thus, in the absence of sufficient cis omega 3 fatty acids in our diet, these fatty acid substitutions take place, the mobility of the GLUT 4 transporters is diminished, the interior biochemistry of the cell is changed and glucose remains elevated in the bloodstream.

Elsewhere in the body, the pancreas secretes excess insulin, the liver manufactures fat from the excess sugar, the adipose cells store excess fat, the body goes into a high urinary mode, insufficient cellular energy is available for bodily activity and the entire endocrine system becomes distorted. Eventually pancreatic failure occurs, body weight plummets and a diabetic crisis is precipitated.

Although there remains much work to be done to fully elucidate all of the steps in all of these pathways, this clearly marks the beginning of a biochemical explanation for the known epidemiological relationship between cheap engineered dietary fats and oils and the onset of Type II Diabetes.

Orthodox Medical Treatment

After the diagnosis of diabetes, modern orthodox medical treatment consists of either oral hypoglycemic agents or insulin.

In 1955, oral hypoglycemic drugs were introduced. Currently available oral hypoglycemic agents fall into five classifications according to their biophysical mode of action.These classes are:

Biguanides Glucosidase inhibitors Meglitinides Sulfonylureas Thiazolidinediones

The biguanides lower blood sugar in three ways. They inhibit the normal release, by the liver, of its glucose stores, they interfere with intestinal absorption of glucose from ingested carbohydrates and they are said to increase peripheral uptake of glucose.

The glucosidase inhibitors are designed to inhibit the amylase enzymes produced by our pancreas and which are essential to the digestion of carbohydrates. The theory is that if the digestion of carbohydrates is inhibited the blood sugar cannot be elevated.

The meglitinides are designed to stimulate the pancreas to produce insulin in a patient that likely already has an elevated level of insulin in their bloodstream. Only rarely does the doctor even measure insulin levels. This drug is frequently prescribed without any knowledge of preexisting insulin levels. The fact that elevated insulin levels are almost as damaging as elevated glucose levels is widely ignored.

The sulfonylurea are another pancreatic stimulant class designed to stimulate the production of insulin. Serum insulin determinations are rarely made by the doctor before prescribing this drug. This drug is often prescribed for type

II diabetics, many of whom already have elevated ineffective insulin. These drugs are notorious for causing hypoglycemia as a side effect.

The thiazolidinediones are famous for causing liver cancer. One of them, Rezulin, was approved in the USA through devious political infighting but failed to get approval in England because it was known to cause liver cancer. The first doctor that had responsibility to approve it at the FDA refused to do so. It was only after he was replaced by a more compliant official that Rezulin gained approval by the FDA. It went on to kill well over 100 diabetes patients and cripple many others before the fight to get it off the market was finally won. Rezulin was designed to stimulate the uptake of glucose from the bloodstream by the peripheral cells and to inhibit the normal secretion of glucose by the liver. The politics of why this drug ever came to market and then remained in the market for such an unexplainable length of time with regulatory agency approval is not clear. As of April 2000 law suits commenced to clarify this situation.[21]

Today insulin is prescribed for both the Type I and Type II diabetics. Injectable insulin substitutes for the insulin that the body no longer produces. Of course, this treatment, while necessary to preserving life for the Type I diabetic, is highly questionable when applied to the Type II diabetic.

It is important to note that neither insulin nor any of these oral hypoglycemic agents exert any curative action whatsoever on any type of diabetes. None of these medical strategies are designed to normalize the cellular uptake of glucose by the cells that need it to power their activity.

The prognosis with this orthodox treatment is increasing disability and early death from heart or kidney failure or the failure of some other vital organ.

The third step to a cure for this disease is to become informed and to apply an alternative methodology that is soundly based upon good science.

Alternative medical treatment

Effective alternative treatment that directly leads to a cure is available today for some Type I and for many Type II diabetics. About 5% of the diabetic population suffers from Type I diabetes; the remaining 95% suffer from Type II diabetes. Gestational diabetes is simply ordinary diabetes contracted by a woman who is pregnant.

For the Type I diabetic an alternative methodology for the

treatment of Type I Diabetes was the subject of intensive research in the early 1990's with several papers presented in the scientific journals. This was done in modern hospitals in Madras, India and subjected to rigorous double-blind studies to prove its efficacy.The protocol operated to restore normal pancreatic beta cell function so the pancreas could again produce insulin as it should. This approach was, apparently, demonstrated to be capable of restoring pancreatic beta cell function where it had been lost. A major complication lies in whether the antigens that originally led to the autoimmune destruction of these beta cells have disappeared from or remain in the body. If they remain, a cure is less likely; if they have disappeared, the cure is more likely.

This early work in Madras India has been continued in a number of laboratories throughout the world and much of it has been published in scientific journals.

If a patent search is conducted to discover research work done on Type I Diabetes that never seems to make it to the marketplace, a number of patents on herbal remedies will be found. These patents typically make strong claims about the regeneration of pancreatic beta cells and the restoring of them to normal function. In particular, patent number 5,886,029 entitled "Method and composition for treatment of diabetes" claims to restore pancreatic beta cell function by regenerating the pancreatic beta cells. This particular patent states in part:

The unique combination of components in the medicinal composition leads to a regeneration of the pancreas cells which then start producing insulin on their own. Since the composition restores normal pancreatic function, treatment can be discontinued after between four and twelve months.

For reasons which, while understandable, are not at all acceptable, this promising line of research never matured and today can be found only in the archives of a few obscure scientific journals and in the patent office. Since absolutely no financial incentive exists to cure type I diabetes, this methodology is not likely to reappear any time soon and certainly not in the American orthodox medical community.

The goal of any effective alternative program is to repair and restore the body's own blood sugar control mechanism. It is the malfunctioning of this mechanism that, over time, directly causes all of the many debilitating symptoms that make orthodox treatment so financially rewarding for the diabetes industry. For Type II Diabetes, the steps in the program are: Repair the faulty blood sugar control system.

This is done simply by substituting clean healthy beneficial fats and oils in the diet for the pristine looking but toxic trans-isomer mix found in attractive plastic containers on room temperature supermarket shelves. Consume only flax oil, fish oil and occasionally cod liver oil until blood sugar starts to stabilize. Then add back healthy oils such as butter, coconut oil, olive oil and clean animal fat. Read labels; refuse to consume cheap junk oils when they appear in processed food or on restaurant menus. Diabetics are chronically short of vitamins and minerals; they need to add a good quality broad spectrum supplement to the diet.

Control blood sugar manually during the recovery cycle. Under medical supervision, gradually discontinue all oral hypoglycemic agents along with any additional drugs given to counteract their side effects. Develop natural blood sugar control by the use of glycaemic tables, by consuming frequent small meals, by the use of fiber, by regular post prandial exercise, and by a complete avoidance of all sugars along with the judicious use of only non-toxic sweeteners. Avoid alcohol until blood sugar stabilizes in the normal range. Avoid caffeine as well as other stimulants; they tend to trigger sugar release by the liver. Keep score by using a pin prick type glucose meter. Keep track of everything you do with a medical diary.

Restore a proper balance of healthy fats and oils when the blood sugar controller again works Permanently remove from the diet, all cheap toxic junk fats and oils and the processed and restaurant foods that contain them. When the blood sugar controller again starts to work correctly, gradually introduce additional healthy foods to the diet. Test the effect of these added foods by monitoring blood sugar levels with the pin prick type blood sugar monitor. Be sure to include the results of these tests in your diary also.

Continue the program until normal insulin values are also restored after blood sugar levels begin to stabilize in the normal region. Once blood sugar levels fall into the normal range the pancreas will gradually stop over producing insulin. This process will typically take a little longer and can be tested by having your physician send a sample of your blood to a lab for a serum insulin determination. A good idea is to wait a couple of months after blood sugar control is restored and then have your physician check your insulin level. It's nice to have blood sugar in the normal range; it's even nicer to have this accomplished without excess insulin in the bloodstream.

Separately repair the collateral damage done by the disease. Vascular problems caused by a chronically elevated glucose level will normally reverse themselves without conscious effort. The effects of retinopathy and of peripheral neuropathy, for example, will usually self repair. However when the fine capillaries in the basement membranes of the kidneys begin to leak due to chronic high blood glucose, the kidneys compensate by laying down scar tissue to prevent the leakage. This scar tissue remains even after the diabetes is cured and is the reason why the kidney damage is not believed to self repair.

A word of warning: when retinopathy develops a temptation will exist to have the damage repaired by laser surgery. This laser technique stops the retinal bleeding by creating scar tissue where the leaks have developed. This scar tissue will prevent normal healing of the fine capillaries in the eye when the diabetes is reversed. By reversing the diabetes instead of opting for laser surgery, there is an excellent chance that the eye will heal completely. However if laser surgery is done, this healing will always be complicated by the scar tissue left by the laser.

The arterial and vascular damage done by years of elevated sugar and insulin and by the proliferation of systemic candida will slowly reverse due to improved diet. However, it takes many years to clean out the arteries by this form of oral chelation. Arterial damage can be reversed much more quickly by using intravenous chelation[26] therapy. What would normally take many years through diet alone, can often be done in six months with intravenous therapy. This is reputed to be effective over 80% of the time. For obvious reasons, don't expect your doctor to approve of this, particularly if he is a heart specialist.

The prognosis is usually swift recovery from the disease and restoration of normal health and energy levels in a few months to a year or more. The length of time that it takes to effect a cure depends upon how long the disease was allowed to develop. For those who quickly work to reverse the disease after early discovery, the time is usually a few months or less. For those who have had the disease for many years, this recovery time may lengthen to a year or more. Thus, there is good reason to get busy reversing this disease as soon as it becomes clearly identified.

By the time you get to this point in this article, and, if we've done a good job of explaining our diabetes epidemic, you should know what causes it, what orthodox medical treatment is all about and why diabetes has become a disgrace both in the US and world wide. Of even greater importance, you have become acquainted with a self-help program that has demonstrated great potential to actually cure this disease.

Thomas Smith is a reluctant medical investigator having been forced into curing his own diabetes because it was obvious that his doctor would not or could not cure it. He has published the results of his successful diabetes investigation in his self-help manual entitled "Insulin: Our Silent Killer" written for the layman but also widely valued by the medical practitioner. This manual details the steps required to reverse Type II Diabetes and references the work being done with Type I Diabetes. In the US, the book may be purchased by sending $29.00 US to him at PO Box 7685, Loveland, Colorado 80537. Outside of the US email us for the special payment and shipping instructions required for international transactions. He has also posted a great deal of useful information about this disease on his web page at: www.Healingmatters.com He can be contacted by email at valley@healingmatters.com and in the US by telephone at: (970) 669-9176

References:

1.   "Fast Stats" National Center for Health Statistics", Deaths/Mortality Preliminary 2001 data

2.   In response to a question from Senator Edward Long about the FDA during US Senate hearings in 1965.

3.   David M. Eisenberg MD, "Credentialing complementary and alternative medical providers", Annals of Internal Medicine, Dec 17, 2002 Vol137 No. 12 p 968

4.   The American Diabetes Association and The American Dietetic Association, "The Official pocket guide to diabetic exchanges", Newly updated; March 1, 1998 McGraw-Hill/Contemporary Distributed Products.

5.   "How do I follow a Healthy diet" American Heart Association National Center, 7272 Greenville Avenue, Dallas, Texas. 75231-4596 americanheart.org

6.   JAC Brown., M.B., B., Chir., "Pears medical encyclopedia, Illustrated", 2071, p-250

7.   Joslyn E.P., Dublin L.I., Marks H.H., "Studies on Diabetes Mellitus", 1933 American Journal of Medical sciences, 186:753-773

8.   Encyclopedia Americana, Library Edition 1966 "Diabetes Mellitus", Vol 9, pp 54-56

9.   American Heart Association, "Stroke (Brain Attack), Aug 28, 1998 www.amhrt.org/ScientificHStats98/05stroke.html American Heart

Association, "Cardiovascular Disease Statistics" Aug 28, 1998 www.amhrt.org/Heart_and_Stroke_A_Z_Guide/cvds.html "Statistics related to overweight and obesity", *www.niddk.nih.gov/health/nutrit/pubs/statobes.htm* and *www.winltdusa.com/about/infocenter/healthnews/articles/obesestats.htm*

10.   Ibid "Diabetes Mellitus" pp 54-55

11.   The veterans administration Coronary Artery Bypass Surgery Cooperative Study Group, "Eleven year survival in the Veterans Administration randomized trial of coronary bypass surgery for stable angina" Veterans Administration co-operative study, New Eng. J Med 1984 311: 1333-1339

Coronary Artery Surgery Study, CASS "A randomized trial of coronary artery bypass surgery: quality of life in patients randomly assigned to treatment groups" Circulation 68 No. 5 1983 :951-960

12.   Trager J., "The Food Chronology", 1995, Henry Holt & Company. N.Y., N.Y. Items listed by date.

13.   "Margarine", Encyclopedia Americana, Library Edition, 1966, pp 279-280

14.   Sally Fallon, MA; Mary C. Enig, PhD, Patricia Connolly; "Nourishing Traditions"; Promotion Publishing, 1995 Mary C Enig PhD, F.A.C.N., "Coconut: In support of Good Health in the 21st Century"; www.live coconutoil.com/maryenig.htm

15.   Bernardo A Houssay MD, et al; "Human Physiology", McGraw-Hill Book Company 1955 pp 400-421

16.   Gustavson J, et al; "Insulin-stimulated glucose uptake involves the

transition of glucose transporters to a caveolae-rich fraction within the plasma cell membrane: implications for type II diabetes." MolMed May 1996, 2(3):367-372

17.   F Ganong MD, "Review of Medical Physiology" 19th edition William, 1999, p-9; pp 26-33

18.   Pan D A, et al; "Skeletal muscle membrane lipid composition is related to adiposity and insulin action", J Clin Invest, 1995 Dec;96(6): 2802-2808

19.   Physicians Desk Reference, 53rd Edition, 1999

20.   Thomas Smith, "Insulin: Our Silent Killer", Rev. 2nd Ed. July, 2000 p20 Thomas Smith, PO Box 7685 Loveland Colorado, 80537, Tel: 1 (970) 669-9176 His website: http://www.healingmatters.com

21.   Law Officies of Charles H Johnson & Associates. Toll free: 1 (800) 535-5727

22.   "Diabetes Mellitus Statistics", American Heart Association, www.amhrt.org

23.   Shanmugasundaram E.R.B., et al, @ Dr. Ambedkar Institute of Diabetes, (Kilpauk Medical College Hospital), Madras. "Possible regeneration of the Islets of Langerhans in Streptozotocin-diabetic rats given Gymnema sylvestre leaf extracts," J. Ethnopharmacology 1990;30:265-279

Shanmugasundaram E.R.B., et al, "Use of Gemnema sylvestre leaf extract in the control of blood glucose in insulin dependent diabetes mellitus", J. Ethanopharmacology, 1990; 30:281-294

24.   Thomas Smith, op. cit pp 97-123

25.   Many popular artificial, sweeteners on sale in the supermarket, are extremely poisonous and dangerous to the diabetic; indeed, many of them are worse than the sugar the diabetic is trying to avoid. see for example: Thomas Smith op. cit. pp 53-58

26.   Dr. Morton Walker, Dr. Hitendra Shah, "Chelation Therapy" 1997, Keats Publishing, Inc. 27 Pine Street (Box 876) New Cannan, Connecticut 06840-0876 ISBN: 0-87983-730-6
Source: Rense.com

China Field Notes

China's rising incomes are expanding its waistlines, the health ministry has found, with 200 million citizens now judged overweight, more than 160 million suffering from high blood pressure and 20 million having diabetes. Weight has piled on in China's shift to more sedentary work in the past 20 years, combined with abundant food and a fattier diet. The report says that since 1992 the number of people considered clinically obese has nearly doubled to 60 million.

Many older Chinese remember the hunger of the 1950s and 60s, when as many as 30 million starved to death. Today fast food restaurants and convenience shops are ubiquitous.

Officials are drafting nutrition guides with the help of the World Health Organization. The deputy health minister said the government would be working hard to educate people about healthier lifestyles.
Source: Guardian Weekly of October 22, 2004.

Chapter 6

<u>Letters of Reference and</u>
<u>Articles About the Author</u>

A Little About The Author

I am a U.S. Navy, World War II Veteran. I was born in New York City and have lived in San Diego for over 50 years. I go dancing regularly and go to the gym every day.

I'm a widower and have a large garden of fruit trees, vegetables, and flowers that keep me busy and outdoors. I started the *Do It Naturally Foundation* because of my concern for the children of our country, especially obese children. I was one of them when I was young and remember the humiliation.

Body and Soul | Keeping Fit

Octogenarian has fun doing it naturally;

Jack Williams, The San Diego Union-Tribune.
San Diego, CA.: Jul 14, 2003. pg. D.3

Max Sturman's beloved backyard garden is an organic buffet, uniting heart and soil. Understandably, he maintains it as assiduously as he does his 85-year-old body.

For 44 years, shaded by 35 fruit trees on a north Clairemont canyon, the garden has provided nutritional bounty. It's also showcased a resourcefulness no less robust than Sturman's health.

Among his innovations: a literal bed of tomatoes, with the cherry red fruit sprouting through the springs of a discarded bed frame; a water-conserving, root-moistening irrigation system; and carpets to shield the soil from the sun.

Only in the last year or so, though, has Sturman become a hard- core missionary for what he calls his "Do It Naturally" diet.

The dedication took on a new dimension when he gave up white flour and white sugar, convinced from research and personal experience that he needed them like he needed another 20 pounds on his modest 5-foot-10, 155-pound frame. Everything in his diet is pretty basic, inspired by the hunters and gatherers who, lacking Krispy Kremes and vending machines, found sustenance from nature.

With supermarket aisles dominated by processed foods, and with newspaper headlines heralding an escalating epidemic of obesity, Sturman found his patience running thin.

So, he woke up one morning and started his mission: a writing project resulting in a 61-page booklet that he called "Do It Naturally: The Diet You Can Live With."

He's given away close to 500 of them over the past year, many to chronically frustrated dieters he encounters daily at his gym in Kearny Mesa. His reward is the positive feedback: a Denny's waitress who dropped six pounds in a week, for example, and the endorsement of a prominent cardiologist, Dr. Dennis Goodman of Scripps Memorial Hospital-La Jolla.

"He is a remarkable gentleman who practices what he preaches," Goodman wrote in the forward of the booklet. "He looks 20 years younger than his age and epitomizes a healthy, well-balanced octogenarian who sets the standards for all of us, no matter your age."

Sturman, who worked such jobs as tool and die maker before retiring from General Dynamics in 1980, expects to live at least as long as his father. "He died at 102 and never ate any sweets," Sturman said.

Sturman's health-consciousness surfaced as a young man. Very ill with ulcers, he went on a vegetarian diet prescribed by a naturopathic physician.

While the regimen cured his ulcers, it left him weak. "I went down to about 135 pounds," he said.

Not until his weight climbed to 200 pounds, much of it seemingly residing in his belly, did he begin to go from one weight-loss scheme to the next. "I tried Atkins, Beverly Hills, the cabbage diet," he said. "When I returned to eating `normally' again, the weight came back."

The culprits, he concluded, were the flour- and sugar-laden treats he now disdains.

These days, eating "normally" is healthy to the max, minus any calorie or fat-gram counting.

Breakfast often is watermelon ("as much as I want"), with lunch and dinner providing animal protein, fresh fruits and vegetables. Tapioca, purchased in an Asian market and sweetened with raisins, is his dessert of choice.

It's plenty enough to fuel a dedicated workout regimen of 1-1/2 to three hours a day, including a Pilates class. That's just mornings. By night, you're liable to find him on the dance floor, taking up a recreation he discovered after knee injuries put a stop to his marathoning.

His preference? "Folk dancing, zydeco and ballroom — with young people," he said.

Sturman can be reached through his Do It Naturally Foundation, 5236 Cole Street, San Diego, CA 92117.

Jack Williams can be reached at (619) 293-1388; by fax at (619) 293-1896; or by e-mail at: jack.williams@uniontrib.com

September 16, 2004

Dear Max:

What a great pleasure to see you again!

I'm spreading the message everywhere!

Best wishes.

Sincerely,

Bob Filner
Member of Congress

Chapter 7

Recipes

SOUPS:

Joe's Chicken Vegetable Soup

Step 1: (broth):
4 chicken breasts (w/skin & bones) or 8 thighs or 1 turkey breast
4 quarts water

Step 2:
2 level tsp salt
1/2 level teaspoon black pepper
1 head of peeled garlic (minced)
1 large yellow onion (1/4" cubes)
1/2 red onion
1 hot pepper, minced (Fresno, Jalepeno or equivalent)
2 pounds red potatoes (1/4" cubes)

1 pound carrots (1/4" cubes)

1 bunch scallions (6-8)

4 stalks celery

1 can of corn with juice, 16-oz

1 red bell pepper

1 yellow bell pepper

Optional: 1 tsp or cube gourmet chicken broth starter.

2 or 3 cans chicken broth, (16oz)

Instructions, Step 1 (broth): Boil meat for 1-1/2 hours to make broth – cool and skim off fat. Remove skin and bones from meat and discard. Cut meat into " chunks, set aside.

Step 2: Add vegetables and spices to soup broth. Add cut up chicken and boil for 1 hour.

Joe's Vegetable Soup

3 quarts broth/vegetable base

1/2 bag green beans

8 oz diced tomatoes

1 beet

1/4 purple cabbage

1/4 tsp black pepper

Optional: 1 can chicken broth 16-oz., 1/4 head broccoli, 1/4 head cauliflower
Boil together for 1 hour.

Hot Borscht

Makes 4 Servings
1 cup tomato juice
1 cup beets, peeled and diced
1 parsnip, diced
2 cups potatoes, diced
1-1/2 cups white cabbage, diced
1 tablespoon safflower oil
2 cloves garlic, minced
1/8 teaspoon vinegar
Pepper to taste
Paprika to taste
Salt to taste
Dill to taste
Parsley for garnish

Combine, in a blender, the tomato juice, beets, parsnip, potatoes and white cabbage. Blend until smooth, adding a little water if necessary. Heat the oil over low heat in a medium sized pot. Sauté the garlic until soft, but not brown. Once the garlic's soft, add the mixture from the blender to the pot. Add vinegar and cook for 20 minutes. Season to taste with pepper, salt, paprika and dill. Ladle soup into bowls and top with the parsley.

Broccoli Soup with Vegetables

Makes 4 Servings
1 cup broccoli
1/2 cup water
1-1/2 cup chicken stock
1/2 cup whole kernel corn, fresh or frozen
1 medium tomato, seeded and cut in thin wedges
1/8 teaspoon lemon juice
Pepper to taste

Place the broccoli florets in a steamer basket and set the basket in a pot with water. Steam the broccoli until it gets bright green. Remove the steamer basket with the broccoli and set aside. Add the chicken stock and corn to the water in the pot and simmer 5 minutes, or until the corn is just tender. Add tomatoes. Chop the broccoli and add it to the pot. Simmer 5 minutes. Add lemon juice, then pepper to taste.

Mexican Style Potato Chowder

Makes 4 Servings

2 tbs safflower oil or butter

1/2 cup diced onion

1/2 cup diced celery

2 tbs arrowroot

1 cup chicken broth

12-oz jar green chili salsa

1/2 cup potatoes, diced

1 tbs fresh parsley, minced

1 tbs fresh basil, chopped

1/2 a bay leaf

1/8 tsp thyme

2 cups potatoes, cubed

Garlic powder to taste

Pepper to taste

Salt to taste

Heat oil over low heat in a medium sized pot. Sauté onion and celery until soft but not brown. Stir in arrowroot and continue cooking over low heat for 2 minutes. Add chicken broth and simmer 3 minutes. Add salsa, potatoes, parsley, basil, thyme and bay leaf. Add Garlic powder, pepper and salt to taste. Simmer until potatoes are tender. Add potatoes and simmer another 5 minutes or until potatoes are tender.

Gingery Chicken Soup

Makes 6 Servings

1-1/2 pounds chicken breasts

6 cups water

1/12 teaspoons salt

3 tbs ginger root, peeled and grated

3 green onions, sliced diagonally

1 cup mushrooms, sliced

8-1/2 oz can water chestnuts, drained and diced

1 tsp soy sauce

1 cup shredded lettuce

In a large pot, combine chicken, water, salt and ginger. Bring to a boil. Then reduce heat, cover, and simmer for about 30 minutes or until chicken is tender. Turn off heat. Remove chicken from pot and let cool slightly. Strain the broth and skim off any fat. Remove skin and bones from the chicken, then cut the meat into 1/2 inch cubes. Turn heat back on and bring broth to a simmer. Add cut chicken, green onions, mushrooms, water chestnuts and soy sauce. Simmer 10 minutes. Stir in lettuce just before serving.

Hot Asparagus Soup

Makes 8 Servings
3 pounds asparagus, fresh or frozen
1/4 pound butter
1 medium onion, chopped
6 cups chicken broth
1/2 tsp ground nutmeg
2 tbs fresh parsley or watercress, chopped

Pepper to taste
Salt to Taste

If using fresh asparagus, wash and remove the tough ends. Slice the asparagus stalks into 2 inch pieces and set aside. In a large, heavy pot heat the butter and sauté the onion until soft (but not brown). Add the asparagus stalk pieces to the pot, setting aside the tips. Cook 1 minute. Add broth, nutmeg, pepper and salt. Bring to a simmer and cook about 18 minutes or until the asparagus stalks are tender.

Add the asparagus tips and cook about 3 minutes or until the tips are tender. Remove some of the cooked tips to use as garnish. Puree the soup in a blender, adding the mixture 2 cups at a time. Serve hot, garnished with parsley and the reserved asparagus tips.

Vegetable Chowder

Makes 8 Servings
1 tbs safflower oil
1 medium onion, sliced
1/2 cup celery, thinly sliced
1 garlic clove, minced
3 cup chicken broth
16oz can tomatoes, undrained and chopped
1 cup carrots, sliced
1 tsp dried basil
1/4 tsp black pepper
1-1/2 cup garbanzo beans/chick peas
1-1/2 cup whole kernel corn, fresh or frozen

1 cup zucchini, sliced

In a large pot, heat oil over medium-low heat. Sauté onion, celery and garlic until soft, but not brown. Add broth, tomatoes, carrots, basil and pepper. Cook for about 25 minutes or until vegetables are tender. Add garbanzo beans, corn and zucchini. Cook for 5 more minutes.

Vegetarian Stew

Makes 4 Servings
1 tbs butter or safflower oil
2 cup mushrooms, sliced thick
1/4 cup chopped onion
1 garlic clove, finely minced
3-4 medium tomatoes, skinned, seeded and cubed
1 medium zucchini, sliced
2 green peppers, seed and cut into 1" chunks
1 tbs fresh parsley, finely chopped
1/2 tsp marjoram
Pepper to taste
Salt to taste
Optional: 1/4 cup white wine

Melt the butter in a large skillet over medium-low heat. Sauté the mushrooms, onion and garlic until tender. Add the remaining ingredients except the wine. Simmer, covered, for 15 minutes or until the vegetable are tender. Add the wine and continue simmering for another 5 minutes.

Persian Lamb and Bean Stew

Makes 8 Servings
2/3 cup dried kidney beans, white kidney beans (cannellini), Great Northern beans or navy beans. [Soaked overnight and drained]
7 cup water
5 tbs butter or safflower oil
1 pound fresh spinach, coarsely chopped
1/3 pound fresh parsley, coarsely chopped
1 cup leeks, finely chopped
1/4 cup green onions or scallions, finely chopped
1 tbs garlic, finely minced
5 tbs olive oil
2 pounds lean lamb, cut into 1" cubes
2 tbs ground turmeric

2-1/2 cups chicken broth, fresh or canned
1/4 cup lemon juice
Pepper to taste
Salt to taste

In a large pot or kettle, bring the beans and water to a boil. Cover and cook until the beans are tender (from 30 minutes to 2 hours, depending on the type of beans). Do not over cook. When the beans are tender, remove from the heat, drain and set aside.

Melt 2 tbs of butter in the kettle/pot over low heat. Add the spinach, parsley, leeks green onions and garlic. Cook, while stirring, the greens are wilted. Set aside.

Heat the olive oil and remaining butter in a skillet. Cook the lamb in the skillet, a few pieces at a time, until browned. (Do not overfill the skillet or the lamb will not brown properly.) As the cubes are cooked, transfer them to the kettle/pot. Add the turmeric, chicken broth and lemon juice to the kettle. Bring the ingredients to a boil, cover, and reduce the heat. Simmer for about 1 hour or until the meat is nearly fork-tender. Add the drained beans, pepper and salt. Simmer for another 10-15 minutes.

ENTREES:

Pinto Beans

1 cup pinto beans
4 cups water
spices to taste
2 celery stalks
2 carrots
1 onion
Boil until soft, blend.

Peppers Stuffed with Barley and Corn

Makes 4 Servings
4 medium, green bell peppers
3/4 cup cooked barley
1/2 cup cooked corn
1 large tomato, skinned, seeded and chopped
1 large scallion, chopped
2 tsp fresh parsley, chopped

1/2 tsp dried basil

1/2 tsp chili powder

Pepper to taste

Salt to taste

Cut tops off the peppers and remove the seeds and membranes. Steam the peppers for 5-6 minutes, then set them aside to cool. To make the pepper filling, mix the remaining ingredients in a large bowl. Once the mixture is complete, stuff the peppers. Place the stuffed peppers in an oiled casserole pan and pour a 1/2 inch of water, stock or tomato juice into the bottom of the pan. Bake, covered, at 350F for 15 minutes. Remove the cover and bake for another 10 minutes. Add more liquid to the bottom of the pan is necessary.

Tomato Lentil Loaf

Makes 4 Servings

2 cups cooked lentils

2 cups tomato sauce

1/2 cup chopped onion

1/2 cup chopped celery

3/4 cup oats

1/2 tsp garlic powder

1/4 tsp Italian seasoning

1/4 tsp celery seeds

Pepper to taste

Salt to taste

Combine all the ingredients in a large bowl. Pack the mixture into an oiled loaf pan, 9x5."

Bake for 45 minutes at 350F. Let cool slightly before removing the loaf from the pan.

Spanish-Style Ground Beef and Rice

Makes 4 Servings

2 tbs safflower oil

2 medium onions, sliced

1 medium green pepper, seeded and diced

3/4 pound ground beef, cooked and drained

2 cups cooked brown rice

3 tomatoes, chopped

2 tbs lemon juice

1/2 cup tomato juice

1/2 tsp pepper

1 tbs onion powder
1/8 tsp garlic powder

Heat the oil in a large skillet over medium-low heat. Sauté the onion and green pepper until soft. Add the rest of the ingredients and combine thoroughly. Simmer 15 minutes.

Bulgarian Bean Salad

Makes 2-3 Servings
2 cups cooked navy beans or kidney beans
1 small green bell pepper, chopped
1 small sweet onion, chopped
1 large carrot, grated
1/4 small head cabbage, shredded
2 tomatoes, chopped
Dressing:
     1 garlic clove, minced
     2 tbs fresh parsley, chopped
     1/2 cup safflower oil
1/4 cup lemon juice
     Pepper to taste
     Salt to taste

In a large bowl, combine the beans and vegetables. Set that aside. In another bowl, combine the dressing's ingredients. Pour the mixed dressing over the salad and toss to coat thoroughly. Chill for 1 hour in the refrigerator to blend the flavors. Serve on romaine lettuce.

Ginger Chicken Salad

Makes 4 Servings
2 tbs butter
1 garlic clove, minced
1" cube ginger, grated
3 half chicken breasts, deboned
2 tbs water
3 cup lettuce, torn
1 cup Chinese cabbage, slivered
1 cup parsley, chopped
1 cup celery, sliced
1/4 cup green onions, sliced
1/2 cup red cabbage, slivered
Optional: 2 tbs sesame seeds
Dressing:
    3 tbs olive oil

1 to 2 tbs lemon juice

1 garlic clove

Dressing: Mix ingredients and let sit a couple minutes. Makes a 1/4 cup.

Salad: Melt butter in a skillet over low heat and sauté garlic and ginger. Cut chicken into bite-sized pieces and sauté in a pot. Add the water and cover the pot, cooking the chicken over low heat until done. Chop vegetables into salad bowl and add the hot chicken. Pour dressing over salad and toss. Sprinkle sesame seeds as garnish.

Poached Fish with Almonds

Makes 4 to 6 Servings

1/2 cup butter

1/2 cup lemon juice

2 tbs dill seed or fennel, fresh or dried

1/4 tbs salt

1/4 tsp black pepper

1 pound fillet of sole, flounder, perch or haddock

2/3 cup whole or slivered almonds

Heat large skillet (or wok) over a medium flame and melt

the butter. Add lemon juice, dill, salt and pepper. Place fish fillets in this sauce. Spoon the sauce over the fish to cook it. Reduce heat to low and poach the fish, cooking it covered for 6 or 7 minutes (until fish flakes easily with a fork). Remove fish to a platter and spoon sauce over it. Sprinkle almonds over the tops.

Onion and Tofu Stir Fry

Makes 3 to 4 Servings
3 tbs oil
2 medium sweet red onions (about 4 cups), sliced in 1/4" rings
1 medium green pepper, cut into strips
1 pound tofu, cubed
1/2 cup water chestnuts, sliced
2 tbs soy sauce
2 tbs lemon juice
1 tsp cornstarch or arrowroot
Sesame seeds

Heat oil in a deep skillet or wok. Add the onions and green pepper and stir fry for about 2 minutes. Carefully stir in the tofu and water chestnuts. Mix the soy sauce with the lemon juice and cornstarch, then add to the skillet/wok. Cover and simmer for 4 to 5 minutes or until heated through. Stir occasionally. Serve over steamed rice and garnish with sesame seeds.

DESSERTS:

Tapioca Pearl (Asian)

8 cups water
1 cup tapioca
1 can coconut cream
1-1/2 cup raisins
1/3 cup unsweetened shredded coconut
1 tbs vanilla
1 tbs almond extract

Boil until tapioca is clear and stir as needed. Add coconut cream, vanilla and almond extract. Mix in the raisins and unsweetened coconut to taste. After your finished, it's best to store the tapioca in small containers with lids because, in time, without a lid the top of the tapioca will become hard.

Compote

6 cups water

1 cup prunes

1 cup raisins

2 apples, chopped

1 pear, cubed

1 cup pineapple chunks

You may use any other fruit, whatever's in season.

Boil until fruit is soft.

Coconut and Sweet Potato Pudding

Makes 6 one cup Servings

4 cup well-cooked (baked or steamed) sweet potatoes

1 cup coconut milk

1 cup shredded coconut, unsweetened or fresh

1 tbs vanilla

Mix in a blender until thoroughly pureed. Pour into glasses and refrigerate until ready to serve.

Coconut Yam Soufflé

Makes 4 Servings

1 large yam (about 2 cups), steamed

1/2 cup coconut milk

1 tsp lemon rind, grated

1/2 cup shredded coconut, unsweetened

2 eggs

1 tsp vanilla extract

Stem the yam (or sweet potato). Separate the egg yolks from the whites and beat the whites until stiff. When the yam is tender, let it cool slightly before peeling. Mash the peeled potato with coconut milk, lemon rind and egg yolks until fluffy. Add the vanilla. Then fold the egg whites thoroughly into the mixture. Pour into a 7" soufflé dish. Bake in preheated 350 oven for 40 minutes.

Enjoy!

Chapter 8
<u>Conclusion</u>

It is very gratifying to know that there are people adapting a healthy lifestyle. I often hear from those who have adapted new habits by reading this book. "DOING IT NATURALLY" they become good, satisfied examples for their peers, families and friends. It's not easy to change one's lifestyle. There are thousands of lobbies in Washington that pour out billions of dollars for their causes and special interests. Corporate America tends to run our country and set up our living and eating habits. Granted, free enterprise is great for our country, but we need provisions. We need healthy changes in the way our government monitors Corporate America. These very industries that provide food, drink and medicine need to give FULL DISCLOSURE of intent to their customers. This would improve our physical and financial health. We would live healthier and curb health care costs. (Those Corporations found guilty of deceiving the consumer or using deceptive practices should be prosecuted to the full extent of the law.) Many people in our country are sick because of all the processed food they consume. If manufacturers would provide healthier food instead of food full of unhealthy preservatives, we would totally benefit. Unfortunately, that is not the case right now. So it is up to us to eat healthy and do it naturally. It is my hope that this trend for "DOING IT NATURALLY" will continue to increase. Everyone, of all ages, needs to watch what they eat. My goal…through this book…is to change the eating habits of our people. Here's to good health!

Max Sturman

Inquires and comments are welcome.
All revenues from this book go to the
Do It Naturally Foundation
to carry on this work.

Do It Naturally Foundation
A NON-PROFIT ORGANIZATION
5236 Cole Street, San Diego, CA 92117

This book is for educational purposes only, we advise you to consult your health care advisor before starting any diet, or lifestyle change.

The Solution

The present epidemics of degenerative diseases of cancer, diabetes, obesity and heart problems are the direct result of our nutrient-stripped man-made foods. The road to recovery will involve an educational program with changes in areas of science, politics, religion, and others where needed. This we must do and we need the help of all the people to see that we succeed which we must if we are to survive. It is true; we were given our choice in how we should live, but it has been misdirected and we have not followed all of the Creator's commandments. The Biblical dietary commandments were health laws meant for our welfare. We have ignored them, and God is angry. His wonderful and fearfully made creation, MAN, has been defiled. These abominations don't go unpunished. The diseases of today, will continue until we change by obeying God's laws.

To accomplish this massive task we will need healthy leaders. There is a correlation between the success of a program and the health of the leaders. Healthcare costs are in the trillions of dollars and are continually rising annually. We desperately need good leadership to organize the operation of reversing the present situation. We will need the cooperation of the government and its appropriate agencies to give direction to reach our goal. <u>Religious leaders</u> need to give sermons that reflect what needs to be done. <u>Doctors</u> must advise their patients what this new information can do to improve their health and prevent disease. <u>Schools</u> need to educate according to this new age lifestyle. In time our civilization will once again follow the biblical dietary commandments, God Given Good Health will prevail.

And God will say, "It is good".

The fact of the matter is there are consequences to polluting your body with harmful foods.
These consequences are the degenerative diseases that are prevalent today.

IT IS OUR OBLIGATION TO TAKE CARE OF OUR BODIES.

A Typical Family Having Their Breakfast

The little child is asking the parents to supply healthy food. How can parents refuse to give their children only the healthiest foods? Start children with healthy foods as soon as possible and they will grow into healthy adults with healthy habits. Teach them the healthy eating plan by repeating the jingle: "No Sugar, No Flour, Will Give Me The Power!" Think about the money you will save through less medical and dental bills when children are not eating sugary foods. This diet can also prevent child and adult diabetes, which is a growing epidemic. Pack healthy lunches for your children to take to school. Include plenty of fresh fruit and vegetables. If children are taught to eat properly from a young age, they will not miss the sweets that damage the health of most children.